A SPIRITUAL TOOL KIT FOR
CHRIST-CENTERED LIVING IN AN
OUT-OF-BALANCE WORLD

A SPIRITUAL TOOL KIT FOR CHRIST-CENTERED LIVING IN AN OUT-OF-BALANCE WORLD

Carolyn Sutton

REVIEW AND HERALD® PUBLISHING ASSOCIATION
HAGERSTOWN. MD 21740

Texts credited to Clear Word are from *The Clear Word,* copyright © 2000, Jack J. Blanco.

Texts credited to Message are from *The Message.* Copyright © 1993, 1994, 1995, 1996, 2000, 2001, 2002. Used by permission of NavPress Publishing Group.

Scripture quotations marked NASB are from the *New American Standard Bible,* copyright © 1960, 1962, 1963, 1968, 1971, 1972, 1973, 1975, 1977, 1994 by The Lockman Foundation. Used by permission.

Texts credited to NIV are from the *Holy Bible, New International Version.* Copyright © 1973, 1978, 1984, International Bible Society. Used by permission of Zondervan Bible Publishers.

Texts credited to NKJV are from the New King James Version. Copyright © 1979, 1980, 1982 by Thomas Nelson, Inc. Used by permission. All rights reserved.

This book was
Edited and Copyedited by Delma Miller
Designed by Candy Harvey
Cover designed by Genesis Design
Cover illustration by Farida Zaman ©Images.com/CORBIS
Electronic makeup by Shirley M. Bolivar
Typeset: Bembo 12/14

PRINTED IN U.S.A.

08 07 06 05 04   5 4 3 2 1

R&H Cataloging Service
Sutton, Carolyn, 1944-
    Staying vertical: a spiritual tool kit for Christ-centered living in an out-of-balance
world.
    1. Christian living.   2. Spiritual life.   I. Title.

                    248

ISBN 0-8280-1813-8

I gratefully dedicate these chapters to my husband,

James H. Sutton,

without whose multifaceted support

this book could *never* have been written!

Jim, as you say to so many others . . . so frequently:

God bless you!

CONTENTS

▲

FALLING OFF THE
BALANCE BEAM

"Many shall run to and fro."
—*Dan. 12:4, NKJV*

"I used to have a handle on life, but it broke."
—*Anonymous e-mail forward*

RECENTLY THE ESPN WEB SITE carried this Associated Press head-line: "U.S. Women Stumble in Preliminaries." The lengthy article de-scribed why the preliminary scores of the women's gymnastics team in Sydney, Australia, were so dismal. One of the main reasons was that "one team member, in her third Olympics, fell off the beam."⋆

It was as simple as that—the young lady just lost her balance.

Maintaining personal balance in a fast-track world is like staying vertical on a balance beam. Just when we think we are successfully managing our busy lives a personal crisis, a deadline, a sudden change in relationship/plans, or an unexpected loss throws us off-kilter and sends us spinning out of control. Often, when we're in that down-ward spiral, we don't even *know how* to go about regaining control.

A counselor once told me he was called to a hospital to visit a highly successful executive. In the hospital room the counselor en-countered a pleasant but weak and emaciated businessman. Various IV tubes were pumping fluids into the man's veins.

"Why are you here in the hospital?" the counselor asked.

"Because I'm malnourished," replied the CEO.

"Why is that?"

"Well, I guess I haven't been eating."

"You guess you haven't been eating?" the counselor repeated, taken aback. "And that would be because—?"

"Well," began the businessman with a sheepish grin, "because I've been too busy to eat." Turning somber, he motioned toward the IV bags beside his bed. "These aren't antibiotics, you know—they're food. To get my system going again."

"So why have you called me?" the counselor asked.

"Because," responded the businessman, "I've been assessing my current state of imbalance. I need help to get my life together again. You see, this is the second time in two years that I've been hospitalized for the very same reason."

And You?

What about you? What does *your* average day look like? Are you in charge of how it unfolds (or is that *unravels*), or is it in charge of you? Do you, as I do, struggle with making resolutions, and then try not to break them as you're swept through life in a rush mode?

So what are we to do when we, like that little gymnast, simply lose balance and start falling?

When Christ was on this earth, He lived in a rush mode, too. Needy people, unexpected emergencies, and routine responsibilities clamored for His time and energy. Even worse, Satan constantly clamored for His soul. Yet everything about Christ's life and presence modeled perfect balance. So in His Son's example, as recorded in the Bible, God gives us a Better Balance Manual, spiritual "tool kit," you might say, for how to stay vertical in an off-kilter world. In studying the words and actions of Christ we can learn the secret of having peace replace our panic and better balance replacing our imbalance.

An action or word of Christ, then, provides the anchor point for each section of this book. By the time you finish Part 1, "Balancing From the Heart," you will have had the opportunity to meditate upon and personally apply four Christ-modeled guidelines for attaining better balance. I would also encourage you to assess your present state of balance/imbalance in the "Homework for the Heart" section at the end of each chapter. You may even wish to write your self-assessments, thoughts, meditations, and prayers in a special journal.

Part 2, "Exercising Our Rights on God's Balance Beam," explores the rights God gives us to "exercise" on life's balance beam.

Christ purchased these rights on our behalf when He died for us on the cross. Exercising them in His strength not only leads us to a deeper intimacy with Him, but also enables us to have a more consistent spiritual walk in these spiritually challenging times.

My prayer is that this journey together will deepen our appreciation for how immeasurably God loves us. May it also open our hearts to the peace and balance only He can bring.

Hey, we may be teetering just a step or two above an off-kilter world, but take heart! God's Word assures us that we don't *have* to fall off the balance beam. We *can* stay vertical!

★ ESPN Web site, Associated Press story, Sept. 17, 2002.

PART 1

▲

Balancing From
the Heart

▲

CHAPTER 1

AVOIDING A CRASH

WHY BALANCE IS IMPORTANT

"Let us lay aside every weight,
and the sin which doth so easily beset us."
—Paul to the Hebrews[1]

"Does your life seem to be out of control? Ask God for help.
He's done a great job with the universe."
—Seen on a billboard[2]

"WOMEN CAN BE STRESSED TO DEATH." This startling headline recently introduced a sidebar in a health journal.[3]

The sidebar briefly explained that researchers, following the medical profiles of 43,000 Japanese women, drew some sobering conclusions. Women with high stress levels are:

- 2.28 times more susceptible to heart diseases than those less stressed.
- 2.24 times more susceptible to stroke.
- 1.64 times more susceptible to death by heart attack.
- More susceptible to hypertension and diabetes (even if they are younger and not overweight).

One of the main reasons personal balance is so important to us is that it keeps us from crashing—on a number of levels.

At the Medford, Oregon, airport a while back I boarded a tiny propeller shuttle—the kind in which people over five feet ten have to stoop a bit in order to walk down the aisle without bumping their heads.

We passengers, sitting mostly toward the front, filled only about eight seats of the 36-seat passenger plane. After the flight attendant shut the door, she stood at the front end of the aisle and momentarily put her fingers in her ears against the noise of the vibrating engines. Then she turned toward us.

I gulped nervously as she called out above the roar, "For the sake of *balance,* could two people please get up and sit anywhere behind row 5?"

Two passengers in front immediately got up and sat down behind row 5. The pilot left his controls momentarily to look out the cockpit door and check on the balance. He nodded his head in approval and squeezed back into his cubbyhole.

The plane took off. We had a turbulent flight to San Francisco, but a safe one.

Having balance in our lives does not guarantee we won't have turbulence. But it does ensure we will have more confident traveling as we journey toward our destination.

New Help From an Old Story

As various apostles chronicled the life of Christ in Scripture, they simultaneously revealed simple—yet profound—principles for living with better balance. Every domain of Christ's life—physical, spiritual, emotional, social, and mental—hung in perfect balance with the other domains. That's why we find in His words and actions principles by which to live our own lives more successfully.

Not long ago I went through a period of time during which I felt as if I were falling off life's balance beam. Events over which I had no control burst into my life with rapid-fire speed. These included several hurried and prolonged out-of-state trips to assist elderly relatives in crisis, the death of my father and two uncles, the stroke suffered by my newly widowed mother, my husband's back-to-back unexpected hospitalizations as he battled unexpected life-threatening illnesses, my own diagnosis and surgery for breast cancer, followed—the next week—by my mother's emergency surgery and nursing-home stay.

In the meantime, of course, previous and ongoing commitments and local church/family responsibilities clamored for my time and attention. As I raced from one emergency to the next, the invisible needle on my energy gauge dropped dangerously low and my feet slipped precariously on the edge of life's balance beam.

I asked God, in my morning devotions, for extra strength and wisdom beyond my years. One morning He answered my plea in a quiet way—while I was rereading a brief, yet familiar, story about Jesus in John 13. I realized this story contained the very information I needed.

It's the story about Jesus in the upper room. What better place could we go with all our stresses, anxiety, and imbalance than into the upper room with Jesus for rest and quiet encouragement?

"Come to Me," He quietly encourages, for He perfectly understands our frenetic pace and frustrated plans. He calls you and me because we are laboring under heavy burdens. He promises that if we join Him, "I will give you rest" (Matt. 11:28, NKJV).

Jesus is the embodiment of peace. The kind of peace you and I so desperately need when yet another crisis blows to smithereens our already-overloaded schedules. Jesus offers the kind of peace we crave when exhaustion causes us to tearfully exclaim, "There's just not enough of me to go around!"

Throughout the upcoming chapters we're going to examine this quiet little story and discover some simple principles—modeled by the Prince of Peace—that will help us to keep moving forward on life's balance beam.

Let's read just the first five verses of this story from John 13.

Verse 1: "It was just before the Passover Feast. Jesus knew that the time had come for him to leave this world and go to the Father. Having loved his own who were in the world, he now showed them the full extent of his love."

Verse 2: "The evening meal was being served, and the devil had already prompted Judas Iscariot, son of Simon, to betray Jesus."

Verses 3, 4: "Jesus knew that the Father had put all things under his power, and that he had come from God and was returning to God; so he got up from the meal, took off his outer clothing, and wrapped a towel around his waist."

Verse 5: "After that, he poured water into a basin and began to wash his disciples' feet, drying them with the towel that was wrapped around him" (NIV).

Notice what Jesus did (verse 4) to prepare for better efficiency at this point in His life. He first laid aside unnecessary "garments," ones that would get in the way of the work His heavenly Father was impressing Him to do at that point in His life.

Unlike us, of course, Christ did not have to lay aside sin in His life, for He had chosen—in the Father's strength—not to yield to it. Yet His "laying aside" or taking off of that which was unnecessary . . . models a principle for us. He rid Himself of whatever would encumber Him, whatever was not absolutely necessary and would only get in His way.

Let's look at ourselves for a moment. Do you and I have any "outer garments" we should consider "laying aside" at this point in our journey? Invisible items of "clothing" that are keeping us in a state of disequilibrium and threatening to "stress us to death," as the magazine article worded it?

You'd be surprised at the unnecessary "clothing" items some of us sometimes pack around! (As you'll see in the next chapter, one of these items for a friend of mine just happened to be a triple-decker, silky-smooth, double-chocolate cake!)

HOMEWORK FOR THE HEART

What habits, obligations, or relational situations (over which I *do* have potential control) have I been allowing to throw me off balance?

Reminder: Studying Christ's words and actions shows us how to better balance our lives—He wants us to be like Him.

(Note: You may wish to keep your responses and reflections to the "Homework for the Heart" exercises in this book in your own loose-leaf notebook or in conjunction with your prayer journal.)

---

[1] Heb. 12:1.

[2] *God Speaks Devotional* (Tulsa, Okla.: Honor Books, 2000), p. 55.

[3] From *Circulation*, in *Vibrant Life*, November/December 2002, p. 7.

CHAPTER 2

▲

BIRTHDAY CAKE DEBACLE

LAYING ASIDE THE NONESSENTIALS

"For fast-acting relief, try slowing down."
—Lily Tomlin[1]

"Let us put aside the deeds of darkness."
—Romans 13:12

AS WITH MANY OF US, my friend, whom I'll call Nicole, battles a sweet tooth. Several years ago she went on yet another diet to lose weight. She had been on this diet only a few days when Mandi, one of her three daughters, had a birthday.

Mandi requested a chocolate cake as part of her family party festivities. Nicole, an excellent cook, baked and frosted a multilayered chocolate fudge cake as the centerpiece of her daughter's birthday celebration.

After dinner that evening everyone ate a large piece of birthday cake. Yet the cake was so tall and so rich that they didn't consume even half of it.

There went my diet, thought Nicole as she put away the food after the party. *Oh, well, I'll start again tomorrow.*

The next day, when Nicole's husband was at work and her daughters at school, Nicole got a hankering for a little taste of chocolate cake.

I can't do that, she thought. *I'm back on my diet today. We-e-e-ell, maybe I could restart my diet after lunch. Just a tiny sliver now won't hurt anything.*

In telling me about this incident several years later, Nicole wryly admitted, "You know how that goes. One sliver leads to another . . . and another . . . and then another."

Nicole didn't stop eating cake slivers until she had devoured the remainder of the cake! Shocked at her impulsive behavior, Nicole panicked. *I don't want my family to think I'm a pig! What do I do now?*

She quickly decided that she would make another cake just like the first one! *Fortunately I still have all the necessary ingredients on hand,* she told herself.

Working feverishly to finish her project before the school bus off-loaded her daughters, Nicole baked—and frosted—another multilayered chocolate fudge cake identical to the first one.

With a sigh of relief she placed it in the newly washed cake holder and beamed at it with a sense of relief. Mission accomplished!

"Oh, no!" she suddenly cried aloud. "My family's going to figure out what I did when they see a *whole,* uneaten cake in there. *Now* what do I do?"

Nicole's first impulse was to cut the cake to the size of the previous evening's uneaten portion. She could simply discard the telltale evidence in a trash bag and throw it in the dumpster.

Nicole carefully chiseled away several large pieces of cake, sliding them onto another plate. With an eye on the kitchen clock, Nicole decided to dispose of them by putting them down the garbage disposal. As she stood above the disposal with the plate of newly baked cake slices, she couldn't help inhaling the fragrance of the rich brown chocolate. She noticed how the glossy dark frosting almost sparkled under the overhead fluorescent lights. Her salivary glands kicked in.

"What a waste!" she moaned audibly. "All those expensive ingredients literally going down the drain! Too bad I can't eat them!"

In the end, she did—and finished rinsing the plate just as her girls walked in the back door after school.

Somehow Nicole's family didn't notice her sluggish manner and peevish temperament that evening. Moreover, they didn't notice the deep guilt she sensed at having failed—once again—to "lay aside" a "garment" that kept her from experiencing better balance.

Our Unnecessary Garments

Like Nicole, who made repeated commitments to eat more

healthfully, we too have made past resolutions, diet-related and otherwise.

Before continuing our discussion, let's take a moment for a brief self-assessment.

HOMEWORK FOR THE HEART

Past Attempts at Balance. What are some "garments" I have attempted to "lay aside" in the past by way of New Year's resolutions or any-time-of-year commitments?

a. _____

b. _____

c. _____

d. _____

e. _____

f. _____

(When you have finished your list, put an X in front of the "garments" you were successful in permanently abandoning or changing for the better. Put a O in front of the ones at which you eventually failed.)

The Key to Restoring Balance. A front-row seminar attendee at one of my seminars was completing the preceding exercise. Suddenly she blurted out, "Oh, my goodness! I have a big fat zero in front of *all* my items. What a failure I've been! No wonder my life is so out of whack!"

The woman sitting beside her quietly remarked, "At least you had the guts to say what I was thinking about *myself*. I just can't seem to get my act together!"

If your X-O ratio faintly resembles that of these two women, please don't become discouraged. Remember that at its core, avoiding that plunge from the balance beam isn't about a self-help program or a rigid personal regimen. Rather, it's about something much more fulfilling: a relationship.

Specifically, it's about a right relationship with Jesus Christ.

On the cross of Calvary He surrendered His life in place of ours so that we would understand that our balance starts in the heart. That is, in *His* heart of love.

How much love does His heart hold for you and me?

"All the treasures of God are opened to you, both the world that now is and that which is to come. The ministry of angels, the gift of His Spirit, the labors of His servants—all are for you. The world, with everything in it, is yours so far as it can do you good."[2]

All of the above is what His love puts at our disposal. Amazing! Indeed, love changes things. More important, God's love changes people. It brings them to places of better balance. In fact, He's the only one who *can* keep us from falling (Jude 24). Only He can give us peace.

So if all of heaven is waiting to help us regain and maintain balance, what is holding us back from *laying aside* the nonessentials in our lives that cause imbalance? What is keeping us from making the necessary changes in our lives?

Perhaps we are afraid to risk changing what we can.

When my neighbor, Karla, changed what she could, it saved her life.

Reminder: We can choose to lay aside nonessentials in order to experience more of God's peace.

---

[1] Lily Tomlin, in *God Always Has a Plan B* (Zondervan, 1999), p. 75.
[2] Ellen G. White, *Thoughts From the Mount of Blessing,* p. 110.

CHAPTER 3

▲

MUGGED BY A COW
CHANGING WHAT WE CAN

*"When you need to make a choice and don't make it,
that in itself is a choice."*
—Anonymous[1]

"It is God who arms me with strength and makes my way perfect."
—2 Sam. 22:33, NIV

"ONE OF MY HEREFORDS HAS BEEN trying to birth a calf for two days,"
explained neighbor Janet over the phone to Karla,[2] our next-door
neighbor. "But she can't seem to get the calf out. You know that
Russ is out of state, and I'm here alone with the cattle. I need help!"

Karla quickly asked, "Have you called a veterinarian?"

"Yes," Janet answered. "He's already here. But he can't maneu-
ver the mama into the squeeze chute to work on her. We need other
people over here to help get her confined so she'll be quiet enough
for him to deliver the calf. Can you and Ted come over and help?"

A few minutes later, at Janet's ranch, Karla and Ted jumped out of
their pickup truck. Three other helpful neighbors had already arrived.

Without incident, the neighbors coaxed and maneuvered the
cow into the squeeze chute where the veterinarian went to work on
her. Perspiration dripping from his face, he tried in vain to extract
the ill-positioned calf.

Finally he wiped his brow, turned to Janet, and said, "I hate to
suggest this, but I fear the calf may already be dead. It may have
started swelling up—which is a possible reason that I haven't been
able to get it out. I need the assistance of another veterinarian. Let
me round somebody up, and we'll be back about 1:30."

Janet pulled the chain that opened a passage from the squeeze chute back into the holding pen. The distressed cow slowly made her way into the pen.

"You might as well go back home," Janet said to her neighbors. "I'll call you this afternoon if the vets need help getting her back into the squeeze chute."

Second Go-round

Early that afternoon the newly summoned neighbors responded to Janet's second call for help. Both vets had pronounced the unborn calf already dead. By now the exhausted cow was suffering noticeably.

"I don't think I can do a C-section," said the first vet, shaking his head, "because of the decomposing calf. I guess we'd better just try to pull it out."

The second vet nodded in agreement. He turned to the assembled neighbors. "Maybe you folks could 'encourage' her back into the squeeze chute."

From outside the fence, which made up the holding pen, Karla and the other neighbors began waving and calling loudly. The unexpected noise and gestures frightened the nervous cow toward the entrance of the squeeze chute. With a lumbering lunge, she entered the chute.

"Good!" exclaimed Janet. "She's in now. Ted, grab that handle over there, and let's move these panels in to hold her tight." The two vets picked up their bags and moved in on either side of the metal panels.

Before Ted and Janet could secure the narrowed pen panels, however, the cow backed up inside the chute. Perhaps vague recollections of her morning ordeal in this very spot flashed through her pain-dulled memory. Whatever the reason, she suddenly lunged forward and then backed up again toward the entrance gate through which she had just exited.

That's when Karla noticed the gate was still open.

"I'll close the gate," Karla said quietly to the others.

"Are you sure it's safe to go in there?" someone asked.

Karla nodded and climbed over the fence into the holding pen.

"I forgot," said Janet, "that gate doesn't have a latch—it's broken."

"That's OK," responded Karla. "I'll secure it with bailing wire or something." Inside the pen now, she strode to the gate, closed it, and then looked about quickly for something with which to secure it.

At that instant the cow animal whirled 180 degrees and exploded through the loosely held gate.

Before Karla could process what was happening, the force of the swinging gate threw her into the corner behind it.

Karla tried to scramble over the fence. But before she could get both feet up on the center fence slat, the cow—head lowered—rammed its 1,200-pound bulk into Karla's back.

"Get it away from me!" Karla screamed. As her neighbors helplessly watched in shock and disbelief, the cow's massive head repeatedly pounded Karla's back and buttocks. Each time the creature attacked, Karla felt as if her right arm, pinned against the fence post, splintered into a million pieces.

Ted grabbed a big stick, shouted, and prodded the crazed cow, hoping the distraction would give his wife an opportunity to escape.

I'm going to die here, Karla thought, *unless something changes real quick!*

Then the cow, weakened by pain, paused to catch her breath.

Should I risk sudden movement in front of the cow? Karla desperately wondered.

Though stunned, Karla put her bruised hands on the top rail of the wooden fence. Friendly hands reached for her swollen arms. The sudden activity, however, energized the cow. Once again the lumbering animal charged into Karla's back, throwing her off balance and pinning her against the corner yet a second time.

"Hang in there, Karla!" Ted shouted. "We'll get you out somehow!" Yet even the veterinarians, used to dealing with large animals, couldn't free Karla. Each bone-crunching attack drowned out the panicked advice and desperate shouts of those beyond the fence.

The Other Side of the Fence

The cow, nearing exhaustion, again paused to catch her breath.

Maybe this is just a nightmare, Karla thought. She tried raising her right arm, but it hung useless. When she tried to lift a leg, the pain shooting through her lower back was debilitating. Staggering from the multiple attacks, Karla realized, *This is my last chance. I've got to change something! I can't worry about what the cow will do.*

She forced her left hand to reach out for a cable supporting the corner post.

Behind her the cow sharply inhaled. Fighting the impulse to remain still, Karla raised her right foot to the middle fence slat.

"She's charging again!" someone cried.

At that instant, the frenzied cow crashed into the corner—missing Karla's right leg by mere inches.

Karla continued making the change she knew she must—her life was at stake. The next thing she knew, she was astride the fence and toppling to the other side as friendly hands eased her fall.

When Karla tried to stand up and walk, she collapsed like a rag doll. Ted dragged her away from the pen while a neighbor ran for ice packs. One veterinarian quickly examined Karla's arm. "I can't believe it," he said, "but I don't think it's broken anywhere." Then he turned his attention back to the suffering cow.

A short time later Karla, covered with blue-black bruises, entered her doctor's office. The medical assistant took one look at her and asked, "What happened to *you?*"

Embarrassed, Karla responded, "I was assaulted by a cow."

After a thorough exam, the doctor told her, "I can't believe you escaped with only big bruises, contusions, and abrasions!"[3]

Although that incident happened some time back, Karla still affirms that if she hadn't changed something when she did, she probably wouldn't be alive today. After all, the cow wasn't going to change. Karla's neighbors and husband couldn't help her. It was up to her—when the opportunity arose—to put her foot on the fence rail and climb out of the pen.

Most of our personal imbalance contexts aren't as dangerous as Karla's. Yet, as with Karla, factors (such as situations and people) that contribute to our imbalance often will not change. Like Karla, *we* must make the decision to change what *we* can when those windows of opportunity open.

So Why Don't We?

So why don't we? Many of us just don't *want* to take the risk. Karla didn't either, at first, because she feared the reaction of the cow. Like Karla, we often prefer to stay in our familiar corner, even though the beast of imbalance pounds away at our waning physical and emotional reserves.

For others of us, a more defining reality exists, which is this.

By nature we are sinful. Therefore, not only are we incapable of making the necessary changes in our lives, many of us are also incapable of even *wanting* to make those changes. Yet, when we don't have the *desire* to change for the better, life goes on as usual—and often for the worse.

Overheard in the Checkout Line

On a Thursday evening some time ago, I overheard an amazing conversation in a rural grocery store checkout line. The exchange occurred between two twentysomethings who didn't know each other. It went exactly like this.

Young man in line behind me to a young woman directly behind him: "You're sure buying a lot of booze. Wow! Five six-packs! You having a party or something?"

Young woman: "No, it's just for my boyfriend and me."

Young man: "Just the two of you are going to drink all *that?*"

Young woman: "Yeah [a little embarrassed], that's what we do on weekends. Find a quiet spot and get drunk."

Young man: "Sounds like a waste of time and money to me. You need to get a life!"

Young woman (nodding sheepishly and pausing): "So what do *you* do on weekends?"

Young man: "Most every weekend my buddy and I go across the state line to Nevada and gamble. It's really fun! Well, actually, we lose quite a bit, sometimes. Suppose I'd better think about changing my hobby before I lose everything."

Making Changes

Most of us know we *should* make some changes in our imbalanced lives. One of my rubber stamps puts it on the line: "If we do not change our direction, we are likely to end up where we are headed."

Maybe we need to change a health-destroying habit through a renewed exercise program or a change in diet. Maybe we need, in God's strength, to replace a negative, energy-sapping attitude with a positive outlook.

Yet, like Karla, we may feel pinned in a corner of gross imbalance while a malicious power, stronger than we, continues its relentless assaults on our lives and on our consciences.

So what can we do?

The answer is . . . nothing, for starters, anyway.

We can't do anything—except redirect our focus to the upper room. There we behold the Man whose every life domain hung in perfect balance with the others. He is our perfect example and our only perfect friend. Only He can give us the *desire* to change, because only He can replace a heart of rebellion (Eze. 36:26) with a repentant heart (Acts 5:30-32) filled with compassion (1 Peter 3:8), love (2 Thess. 3:5), peace (John 14:27), and the willingness to be balanced in Him (Rom. 1:5).

What John reveals about Christ in the upper room (John 13:1, 3) not only gives us hope despite our chronic imbalance but also provides the key to effective *motivation* behind positive change.

HOMEWORK FOR THE HEART

Motives for Change, Part 1. Each of the following texts offers a spiritually based motive for positive decisions/choices/changes made by a well-known Bible character. Note the context of each verse or passage and the person's choice for better balance. Then identify the underlying motive in each case.

Joseph

Context and choice (Gen. 39:9): _____

Motive: _____

Moses

Context and choice (Heb. 11:24-26): _____

Motive: _____

Esther

Context and choice (Esther 4:14-16): _____

Motive: _____

Daniel

Context and choice (Dan. 1:8): _____

Motive: _____

Jesus

Context and choice (Mark 14:35, 36): _____

Motive: _____

Why not pause a few moments right now to reflect on a balance-enhancing change you sense the Savior has impressed you to make? Request His help in identifying a God-honoring motive for making such a change.

Motives for Change, Part 2. Think about asking Him to reveal any negative condition in your heart that might be blocking His Spirit from giving you the *desire* to make balance-enhancing changes in your life. The Bible reveals a number of conditions that can keep us from *wanting* to make changes, or that keep God from changing us. Here are some of them.

- Selfishness/self-centeredness (Rom. 15:1-3; 2 Tim. 3:2, 5)
- Pride (Prov. 8:13; Mark 7:22, 23; 1 Tim. 3:6; 1 John 2:16)

- Desire to please people over pleasing God (Eph. 6:6; Col. 3:22; James 4:4)
- Hardness of heart based on unbelief (Heb. 4:6, 7)
- Putting one's own wisdom above that of God's (Rom. 1:21, 22)
- Harbored anger/bitterness (Matt. 5:22; Eph. 4:26, 31; Col. 3:8)
- Cherished/hidden sin (Ps. 66:18; Isa. 59:2)
- An unforgiving spirit (Mark 11:25, 26; Luke 11:4)
- Refusing to accept a love of the truth (2 Thess. 2:10, 11)

If you have identified any of the above conditions in your heart and don't want it there any more, Peter offers the ultimate solution. When listeners, in response to his sermon, asked what they could do about conditions in their lives that had them off balance, he answered, "Repent." Then he quickly added the assurance that God would immediately send His Holy Spirit to help them in their walk toward better balance (Acts 2:37, 38).

Today the loving Father is so very willing to do the same for us. Why not ask Him now to give you the *desire* to do what He's impressed you to do? He's only a prayer away.

Reminder: God will enable us to repent and will give us the desire to make positive balance-enhancing changes in our lives.

---

[1] E. C. McKenzie, compiler, *14,000 Quips and Quotes for Speakers, Writers, Editors, Preachers, and Teachers* (Grand Rapids: Baker Book House, 1980), p. 76.

[2] Not their real names.

[3] Unfortunately, the poor cow didn't fare so well. The prolonged carriage of a decomposing calf in her womb led to her death later that day.

▲

CHAPTER 4

IT'S A LOVE THING

BETTER BALANCE PRINCIPLE 1

"Be still, and know that I am God."
—Ps. 46:10

"He will quiet you with His love."
—Zeph. 3:17, NKJV

AT THE CLOSE OF THE PREVIOUS CHAPTER we mentioned that John revealed something about Christ in the upper room that provides the key to right motivation behind positive change in our lives.

Have you ever heard someone use this expression about another person: "to know him is to love him"?

This statement applies to God, as well. To truly know God is to love Him.

A rereading of John 13, verses 1 to 4, shows us that this was Christ's experience with His heavenly Father. Notice how John uses forms of both *know* and *love* in describing Christ's relationship with His Father.

"Now before the feast of the Passover, when Jesus *knew* that His hour had come that He should depart from this world to the Father, having *loved* His own who were in the world, He *loved* them to the end. . . .

"Jesus, *knowing* that the Father had given all things into His hands, and that He had come from God and was going to God, rose from supper and laid aside His garments" (NKJV).

John makes reference to the fact that Jesus knew or understood what God had done for Him—and was continuing to do in Him.

Christ knew the heart of His Father because He had spent so

much time with Him in prayer and, obviously, in Scripture meditation (as He always had just the right Scripture reference on the tip of His tongue for any given situation).

Knowing His Father so well, Christ couldn't help understanding His love—the very love the Son came to demonstrate to us.

His response to this divine love was to love His Father in return. That's how it works between two people, isn't it?

Bed of Roses

One Saturday evening during my single years I drove into the shadowy church parking lot. From behind the steering wheel of my little secondhand Ford, I watched life unfolding just beyond the double-glass doors. Smiling parishioners, the majority wearing red, carried plates of food from the kitchen into the fellowship hall. On a distant counter I could see what appeared to be a pile of long-stemmed red roses.

Having recently moved to Oregon, I still felt a bit out of place in this new church family. How I wished I hadn't told Agnes (not her real name) I *might* show up for the church Valentine's Day social. I also wished I weren't still feeling so alone. So insecure. So just-turned-50. So . . . divorced.

I caught a glimpse of Agnes scurrying into the fellowship hall. Her 60-plus years of life hadn't been a bed of roses. Loss of loved ones and severe back pain headed her list of woes. Yet she always managed such a warm, welcoming smile

I shivered as a frosty chill crept into the car.

Next I saw silver-haired Jim walk past the doors carrying some type of glass container. Snatches of conversation I'd overheard indicated this gentleman was also struggling to pick up the pieces of his life. Though not understanding why God had led him down a recent thorny path, this new Christian was coping with tragedy by getting to know God better. I respected that. I also respected his quiet acts of kindness to those in need that I'd also heard about.

Suddenly I felt ashamed. If Agnes and Jim—who'd suffered much greater losses than I—could celebrate this love-centered holiday with smiles on their faces, what was my problem?

When I entered, Eula flashed a friendly smile at me and steered me toward a chair at the end of a table. We had to squeeze past Jim, who was busy stuffing an armload of long-stemmed roses into a widemouthed vase.

I enjoyed the evening in spite of myself.

Just before the benediction, Agnes's husband, Dave (not his real name, and the evening's emcee), announced, "We have something special for the ladies tonight. Big Jim here has brought a red rose for every girl here—whether she's 8 or 80." Dave continued, "I understand Jim had to run all over town in order to find enough roses for y'all."

As Agnes helped Jim pass out the roses, I tried to remember the last time someone had given me a rose—but couldn't.

"Here's one for you," said Jim, thrusting a perfect bloom in my direction.

Three days later when the rose began to droop on its stem, I considered throwing it in the trash. But that didn't seem like the right thing to do. Instead I hung it upside down from a lamp and let it dry.

Four months later when I drove out of state to start a new job on the East Coast, the dried rose was suspended from my rearview mirror. I *still* didn't know what to do with it. The night before I moved, Jim had phoned saying, "I know you're not ready for a relationship yet, but I'll keep you in my prayers. But may I keep in touch? If and when you're ever comfortable with the idea, may I fly to Maryland and take you out to dinner some evening?"

I hadn't been quite sure how to answer.

Four hundred miles into my cross-country trip I stopped briefly at the cemetery where my maternal grandmother is buried. I stood beside her gravestone and read its inscription: "She lived for others."

The inscription on Gram's tombstone reminded me of someone else who "lived for others." When I drove away a few minutes later, the dried rose lay across Grandma's gravestone, its stiff stem securely tucked into a thick grassy tuft to hold it in place.

Though I'd finally decided what to do about the rose, I still didn't know what to do about Jim.

Nearly a year later I agreed to his earlier proposed visit—and then to subsequent visits. I must admit I didn't fall in love with him for a long time. Rather, I fell in love with his helpful ways, his kindness, his thoughtfulness, his sense of humor. Most of all, I fell in love with the way he was growing to know and appreciate the Savior.

On Valentine's Day, exactly two years after he had given roses to all us "girls" in that little Oregon church, Jim and I purchased a wedding license in a Maryland courthouse. That same afternoon— before Jim arrived from his hotel room to pick me up for dinner— a local florist delivered a single red rose. The accompanying card read, "For my future bride."

I met Jim at my front door with a hug and words of gratitude for the beautiful rose. He looked at me a long time before speaking, a twinkle behind the tears in his eyes.

"Haven't you figured it out *yet?*" he asked. "I'm marrying you because it's going to be a whole lot cheaper than if I don't."

"What do you mean?" I asked.

"Now I have to pay for only one rose."

Trying to control the emotion in his voice, Jim asked, "Do you remember the valentine's social when I'd run all over town trying to find enough roses to give one to each of the church ladies?"

"Yes."

"Well, even back then I suspected I wanted you in my life, but the time wasn't right for either of us. I didn't want to blow it for us before things even had a chance to really get started. So I took the risk . . . and shelled out $240 in order to be able to give *you* a single rose that evening."

Tears filled my eyes.

The man to whom I'd just entrusted the second half of my life leaned over to kiss me. He held my face between his hands. "Four dozen roses may have gone to four dozen different homes in Oregon that night, but darlin', that bed of roses was all for *you!*"

To Know Him Is to Love Him

This bit of information about the workings of my future bridegroom's heart only increased my love for him.

Likewise, the better we know and understand the heart of our heavenly Father, the more we will want to spend the rest of our lives with Him. The main way Christ loved His Father back was by making choices within His Father's will (Ps. 40:8).

In the upper room that particular evening, Jesus sensed that His Father's will was for Him to serve the disciples. So He changed, out of *love* for His Father, what He needed to in order to accomplish His Father's will in the most balanced way possible. As we already know, the first step was to lay aside His outer garments.

This brings us to our first Better Balance Principle.

Better Balance Principle 1

I will experience lasting changes toward better balance in my life when my desire to change is based on a *love* response to Christ for what He has done for me and still wants to do for me (John 3:16; 14:15, 21).

In his book *The Pursuit of God* A. W. Tozer states, "We can exaggerate about many things; but we can never exaggerate our obligation to Jesus, or to the compassionate abundance of the love of Jesus to us."★

No doubt about it—the right motivation behind positive change in our lives has to do with how well we know Christ. It's definitely a love thing!

HOMEWORK FOR THE HEART

What do I know for certain that God—out of love—has done for me?

Reminder: Knowing and loving God is where any lasting positive change begins.

★ A. W. Tozer, *The Pursuit of God,* pp. 54, 55.

CHAPTER 5

▲

PARACHUTING CATS

To Know Him Is to Appreciate My Value

"You . . . are acquainted with all my ways. . . .
You have hedged me behind and before, and laid
Your hand upon me. Such knowledge is too wonderful for me."
—King David[1]

IN THE PREVIOUS CHAPTER WE DISCUSSED the importance of knowing God. For "to know Him is to love Him."

However, have you considered recently how well God knows *you?* In Psalm 139:14, King David praised God for making him "fearfully and wonderfully." David recognized the fact that God had created him as a unique individual.

How long has it been since you praised God for creating you as the invaluable one-of-a-kind work of art that you are?

How easy for us to pick out our flaws, weaknesses, and idiosyncrasies rather than notice the special characteristics with which God crafted us as individuals—unique from one another.

Some of us have difficulty believing that, flawed as we—and our circumstances—are, God can still bring better balance to our lives. He still wants us in His service.

Let me illustrate. In 1954 the British Royal Air Force "drafted" two cats.[2] That's right—cats! These cats were drafted to make a test parachute jump from an altitude of 350 feet.

You see, deep in the Malayan jungle mice were overrunning a British fort. Commanders of this garrison had relayed an urgent call for help because the tiny rodents were destroying the fort's food supply. That's why the RAF airlifted feline paratroopers into the "battle zone."

Now, cats have unique characteristics: they move silently, they see well in the dark, they are excellent predators, and they live through so many dangerous encounters that some people joke that cats have "nine lives." Throughout the centuries, however, these very characteristics have caused cats to be among the most misunderstood of any creatures in the animal kingdom.

For example, ancient Britons believed cats could cure blindness because they see so well in the dark. Russians used cat skins to treat stomach cramps.[3] During the Dark Ages—again because of their special characteristics—cats were associated with witchcraft, hunted down, and killed along with their owners.

Yet the very characteristics that made some people misunderstand cats—their silence, their predatory skills, their survival instincts—were the *very* characteristics that made them the perfect choice to execute a special mission for the British Royal Air Force. One might say that the British Royal Air Force "redeemed" these oft-maligned feline idiosyncrasies for their own noble purposes.

God also gave you and me special, unique characteristics. Perhaps our individual characteristics are so unique that others have sometimes misunderstood them. Or even singled them out for ridicule.

Yet God has a plan for your life and mine. And His plan includes the individuality with which He has created each of us.

Knowing God Better

Since the purpose of this chapter is to encourage an examination of God's unique involvement in our personal lives, we will be reflecting, assessing, and responding more here than in most other chapters.

As you respond to the following thought prompters, remember that, first and foremost, God made you *uniquely . . . you!*

Now open your Better Balance notebook, which I hope you have started. Turn to the next page and entitle it "What Makes Me Unique."

By the time you finish responding to the following thought prompters, I trust you will have a more specific picture than before of how God has been at work in your life—not to mention reminders of His tender regard toward you.

Before responding, however, open your Bible and prayerfully read Psalm 139.

Now, with that magnificent psalm fresh in your mind, respond to the following thought prompters.

"What Makes Me Unique"

1. Who I already am. (List *all* the roles you currently assume in your life, such as daughter, wife, mother, nurse, accountant, grandmother, college graduate, home/foreign missionary.)

2. My natural abilities and positive inclinations. (List as many as possible, including natural talents, such as being musical, compassionate, athletic, a good organizer, a budget-balancer, artistic, someone who memorizes easily, a gardener, someone with the ability to sense the unspoken needs of others.)

3. My actual developed skills and gifts. (For example, parenting, playing the saxophone, speaking a foreign language, telling stories, chairing a committee, teaching children.)

4. My God-given resources. (Time, physical energy, financial resources, spiritual resources and gifts, possessions, types of income.)

5. Activities I enjoy because they help me grow on some level. (For example, gym workouts three times a week, reading, scrapbooking, giving Bible studies, visiting shut-ins, participating in a musical group or outdoor sports.)

6. Ways I could meet my own needs while meeting the needs of others. (For example, singing in a church choir if I have music abilities; being a volunteer art teacher at a local school if I'm artistic, etc.)

Understanding God Better

You now have tangible evidence (knowledge) of ways in which God has been at work in your life through faithfulness and blessings.

Referring back to your responses, reflect (in writing, if you wish) how this documented "knowledge" of God's involvement in your life might help you better understand *who* God is.

For example, your responses to "Who I already am" might indicate to you that God created us to be social beings who interact with one another. Therefore, He is a God of interaction, of relationship.

Your "natural abilities and positive inclinations" responses may suggest that God equips each of us with abilities and talents that add richness to our lives.

From this perspective, you might conclude that God is a being who delights in variety and endless possibilities—yes, even through *you*!

Your responses to "my developed skills and gifts" furnish undeniable evidence of God's guiding hand in your life. Therefore, He is a God of personal involvement.

Your "God-given resources" responses may include, for example, the fact that God worked a few financial "mini-miracles" so that you could obtain a college education. What might this and other providences on your behalf demonstrate about God's blatant grace toward you?

Better Understanding

Jeremiah recorded these words of God's. "Let not the wise man glory in his wisdom, let not the mighty man glory in his might, nor let the rich man glory in his riches; but let him who glories glory in this, that he *understands* and *knows* Me" (Jer. 9:23, 24, NKJV).

These verses strongly imply that our primary cause for celebration can never be based on how blessed, talented, or financially stable we are. Rather, our main reason to "glory" is that we *know* and *understand* God.

When our hearts and minds are filled more and more with the knowledge and understanding of God, how should we respond to His lovingkindness on our behalf?

Take a moment to answer the following questions.

- Where do I suspect God wants me to be and/or be doing three years from now?
- What might I need to change/do in order for the above to become a reality?
- What have I recently felt that God has been laying on my heart about making some positive changes in my life?
- Am I willing to allow Him to help me make these changes?

During the course of this chapter you have completed a very informal personal assessment concerning God's faithfulness in your unique situation.

In the final thought prompter that you answered, you also had an opportunity to think about how you might like to respond to God's goodness in a focused and ongoing way.

What About My Inadequacies?

While responding to the preceding thought prompters, some of us may have been tempted to feel as if God can't really help us work toward better balance. We feel this way because of a rough childhood. Or unfair, cruel events in our lives perpetrated by people over whom we had no control. Others of us may be doubting God's care because of an ongoing uncertainty or a lingering illness. As a consequence, we feel as if we have nothing to offer others because of who we are *not*.

Oh, but let's not allow these things to destroy our hope of someday being securely and perfectly positioned on top of life's balance beam! For God, in His Word, has a reminder for us who struggle with what we are not. In fact, we cannot surprise, shock, or discourage Him with information about who we are. He already knows and has been working on our behalf anyway.

In Psalm 139, David said, "O Lord, thou hast searched me, and known me. . . . How precious also are thy thoughts unto me, O God! how great is the sum of them!" (verses 1-17).

God understands our disappointments and weaknesses so much better than we do. Don't you find it amazing that despite our inadequacies, God's thoughts toward us have always been "precious"? In fact, they were so precious that they culminated in a special mission.

The British Royal Air Force chose cats for its special mission. When God, however, planned a destiny-determining mission to complete on *our* behalf, He chose His only Son. Because of *His* unique characteristics, Jesus Christ was the only agent who could bring this mission to fruition.

He was the only one who could live a perfect life and then offer Himself as a perfect sacrifice in our stead by dying on the cross.

The accomplishment of that unspeakably significant long-ago mission gives Him the right to receive us in our state of imbalance—today. If we are falling off the balance beam, He invites us to fall straight into His arms so that He can redeem our inadequacies, idiosyncrasies, disappointments, and failures.

Every time we turn to Him, He shows us the way to better balance. "In returning and rest shall ye be saved; in quietness and in confidence shall be your strength" (Isa. 30:15).

God has promised to redeem everything that's out of whack in our lives, both for His glory and for our highest good! He is in the personal redemption business.

Back to the Upper Room

That's why Christ gathered 12 unbalanced disciples about Himself in the upper room so long ago.

Good old shoot-from-the-lip Peter

Political activist Simon

Jealous John

Fiery-tempered James

Doubting Thomas.

Yet Jesus was calling them out of imbalance because He was about to entrust them with a very urgent mission—that of taking His gospel to the world.

Because of their unique characteristics the British Royal Air Force chose cats to carry out a special task no one else could accomplish.

Despite, and because of, their unique characteristics, Jesus chose a motley array of off-kilter men to carry out His precious mission.

So who knows? Maybe *your* unique characteristics will make you the perfect choice for some of God's special missions as well!

HOMEWORK FOR THE HEART

What He's Done for Me. At your earliest convenience, read the first three chapters of Ephesians. Not only do the first three verses affirm that God has *chosen* you (because He loves you), but these chapters are, in effect, a "bank statement" itemizing more than

20 priceless deposits He's made to your account.

Reminder: Better understanding how God has worked through—and despite—our uniqueness helps us better understand how much He values us.

---

[1] Psalm 139:3-6, NKJV.

[2] Leonore Fleischer, *The Cat's Pajamas* (New York: Harper and Row, 1981), p. 131.

[3] *Ibid.*, p. 132.

CHAPTER 6

▲

CONQUEROR OF THE INTERIOR
BETTER BALANCE PRINCIPLE 2

"Teach me your way, O Lord, and I will walk in your truth."
—Ps. 86:11, NIV

"Nature gives man corn, but man must grind it;
God gives man a will, but man must make the right choices."
—Unknown[1]

FOLLOWING A SHORT-TERM MISSION TRIP to Micronesia, my husband and I had the opportunity of spending one week in Queensland, Australia. While there, I learned about a very significant eighteenth-century Aboriginal guide, known by the name of John Piper.[2]

This uneducated man had rendered invaluable service to a European exploration party. Not only had he led them through the wild, uncharted territories of the Australian interior, helping procure both geographical guidance, indigenous foods, and water for the explorers, Piper had also kept them alive by locating water for the team. As one explorer said years later, "Without a guide in such country one is almost powerless."[3]

The explorers realized that their expedition culminated in resounding success, largely owing to the efforts of Piper.

In appreciation they showered him with gifts: an old gun, blankets, a red coat, and a feathered hat once worn by a governor. As a last token of appreciation, the explorers attempted to give Piper a brass breastplate engraved with the title "King."

The Aborigine shook his head, respectfully declining.

Then, unexpectedly, he said, "I want it to read 'Conqueror of the Interior.'"

Loving Him Back

I don't know about you, but almost every New Year's resolution I've made, nearly every "garment" I've ever tried to "lay aside," practically every sin I've endeavored to abandon has been *my* attempt to become a "conqueror" of my carnal interior.

How my conscience resonates with this quote from the book *Steps to Christ:* "You desire to give yourself to Him, but you are weak in moral power, in slavery to doubt, and controlled by the habits of your life of sin. Your promises and resolutions are like ropes of sand. You cannot control your thoughts, your impulses, your affections."[4]

Any unconquered thought, impulse, or affection will always cause imbalance in our lives. Let's continue the above quote.

"What you need to understand is the true force of the will. This is the governing power . . . , the power of decision, or of choice. Everything depends on the right action of the will. The power of choice God has given to men; it is theirs to exercise. You cannot change your heart, you cannot of yourself give to God its affections; but you can choose to serve Him. You can give Him your will; He will then work in you to will and to do according to His good pleasure."[5]

In a previous chapter we discussed how the old adage "To know him is to love him" certainly applies to our relationship with God. For when we study and meditate on what He has done—and is doing—for us, the natural heart response is to love Him in return.

Jim began loving me long before I loved him. In many small ways he demonstrated his love. Over time, as I got to know him better and continued to be the object of his kindnesses, I couldn't help loving him back—and eventually married him.

Because I love him so much now, I truly want to please him, even when doing so inconveniences me. Since I know him well enough now to understand what makes him happy, I can make the choices that will cheer his heart. This is the best way I know of loving him back—for loving me, in the first place.

Likewise, the better we understand what makes the heavenly Father happy, the more *willing* we will be to make choices that cheer His heart.

In 2 Corinthians 8:12, Paul emphasizes that *wanting* to make choices that please God is where better heart balance *begins*. Paul said, "If there be *first a willing* mind . . ." Only love for God can make us a conqueror of the interior—which brings us to our second Better Balance Principle.

Better Balance Principle 2

True balance, in both our character and lifestyle, can occur only when we continually submit our wills to the will of our loving God (Phil. 2:12, 13).

Let's review that final thought prompter from the previous chapter: Am I *willing* to allow God to help me make changes that will not only please Him but also bring better balance to my life?

Let's continue the self-assessment we began in previous chapters. Open your Better Balance notebook and respond to the following thought prompters.

Areas in Which I Most Need God's Help to Change

- In what area or areas do I most feel the need of God's help for change?
- Is my imbalance caused by my having taken on more responsibilities than I realistically have time for? If so, how? (Some of us have a tendency to let other people's emergencies become our urgencies. In our well-meaning responses, though, we sometimes lose *ourselves* in the scramble to "be there" for everyone else.)
- Do I have a self-control issue at stake?
- Is my "time with God" at the top of my daily schedule or elsewhere?
- What things (or what individuals) have I been letting slide lately?
- Have my priorities become scrambled for one reason or another?
- Is my stress level out of control? Have I been doing anything about it?
- Have I been neglecting some area of my life?

Before you, in desperation, throw out your Better Balance notebook, take another look at Jesus in the upper room. Specifically, let's return to John 13:4.

After Jesus had laid aside His unnecessary garments, He "took a towel, and girded himself." In place of what He had taken off, He put something on.

He put on only that which was needful for Him to accomplish—and please—His Father's will at that moment in time. For the purposes of our discussion in this book, we could say that Christ equipped Himself with what was essential to living a balanced and useful life.

Because of His love for us, Jesus would wrestle (*three* times inside the next hour!) with whether to do His own will or the will of His Father (Matt. 26:39, 42, 44). This personal dilemma concerning Better Balance Principle 2 was the epicenter of Christ's great struggle in the Garden of Gethsemane.

Praise God that He chose to do His Father's will! And praise God that Jesus will enable us to do the same!

HOMEWORK FOR THE HEART

Consider talking to God about your desire to submit, first and always, your will to Him—from this point on.

After looking over your responses to this chapter's thought prompters about what contributes to imbalance in your life, tell God what you are *willing* to "lay aside."

As for what you might "put on" in its place, let's rendezvous in the next chapter for some suggestions from God Himself.

"Dear God, thank You for the example of hope and order lived out by Jesus when He was on this earth. We are so grateful that we don't have to generate positive balance-enhancing choices on our own. Our even being *willing* to exercise our God-given power of choice to please You is exciting evidence that You're already at work within our hearts [1 John 4:4].

"We are eternally grateful that our choices aren't what will save us. Rather, *Your* choices on our behalf—*if* we accept them—already have! In the name of Your dear Son we pray, amen."

Reminder: Better balance starts when, trusting God's love for us, we place our wills (our power of choice) in His hands.

---

[1] E. C. McKenzie, *14,000 Quips and Quotes*, p. 76.

[2] Henry Reynolds, *Black Pioneers: How Aboriginal and Islander People Helped Build Australia* (Victoria, Australia: Penguin Books Australia, Ltd., 2000), p. 28.

[3] *Ibid.*, p. 17.

[4] Ellen G. White, *Steps to Christ*, p. 47.

[5] *Ibid.*

CHAPTER 7

▲

"PUTTING ON" THE ESSENTIALS

BETTER BALANCE PRINCIPLE 3

"He . . . took a towel, and girded himself."
—John 13:4

"A Christian is one who makes it easier
for other people to believe in God."
—Unknown[1]

WHILE DRIVING HOME THE OTHER DAY via Oregon's Interstate 5, I got stuck behind a big rig laboring up a steep hill. In an effort to defuse my growing irritation over this unexpected delay, I began reading everything written on the back of the truck, starting with the license plate and moving on from there.

Plastered somewhere in the lower left quadrant of the rear trailer door was this blatant notice. It not only caught my eye but also gave me pause for reflection.

"I'm a professional driver," it stated. "My conduct and driving skills are on display. If you have any comments, please phone 1-800- . . ."

When I finally had the opportunity to pull out into the passing lane in order to get around the semi, I chose not to. Instead (since the posted notice had invited me to do so), I stayed where I could assess this driver's "conduct and driving skills."

Between Rogue River and my off-ramp seven miles later, the driver of that rig did nothing to suggest that he was anything other than a seasoned professional with courteous motoring conduct and precautionary driving skills.

Traveling His Road

While driving behind that big rig, I also reflected that whatever I choose to "put on"—in an attempt at better balance—is also "on display."

The apostle John states that if we *say* we abide in Christ (in other words, if we claim to be "professional" Christians), then we will walk (or "drive") as He did (1 John 2:6).

In addition to the towel with which Christ girded Himself in the upper room, what other attributes or "garments" did His disciples see on display as He prepared to minister to them that evening?

They observed the same "garments" God wants to put on us. Here is a partial list:

- *Contentment* for whatever blessings we have (2 Cor. 12:9, 10; Phil. 4:11-13).
- *Faith* that trusts Him to supply all our needs (Phil. 4:19; Rom. 8:28).
- *Loving forgiveness* toward those who have wronged us (Luke 6:27; 1 Cor. 2:8-11; Eph. 4:32).
- *Moderation* in—or elimination of—imbalance-causing elements such as harmful food items, immoral entertainment/reading matter, or a workload that is much too heavy for our bodies and minds to bear (Eccl. 3:1; Phil. 4:5, 8).
- *Praise* instead of anxiety and worry (Phil. 4:4, 6; 1 Thess. 5:18).
- *Assurance* that He is bigger than any fear, problem, or enemy of ours (1 John 4:4; Isa. 49:25; 59:19; Prov. 1:33; 29:25; 2 Tim. 1:7-9).
- *Likeness to God's holy character* as the top priority and pursuit of our hearts (Matt. 6:33; Rom. 13:14).

Working With What We Still Have

Some of us, however, may feel that we have lost so much through being imbalanced (often through our own faulty choices) that we don't deserve Christ's help in putting our lives in order again.

May I suggest (based on Scripture) that when we are falling off the balance beam is precisely the best time for us to reach out for His steadying hand.

What more could possibly go wrong when we surrender to Him

what we are about to lose anyway? Especially when our Creator is such a master at creating order from chaos.

When a famine-stricken widow and her little boy submitted the last of their flour and oil in order for God's prophet to have a loaf of bread, the Lord surprised them with a continuous supply of these two staples until the worst of the famine was over (1 Kings 17:8-16).

When a little child surrendered his meager noontime sack lunch to the Savior, Christ expanded it into a potluck for a hungry 5,000-plus-member congregation (Luke 9:12-17). Said Watchman Nee, the renowned twentieth-century Chinese spiritual leader and martyr, "The point was not the quantity of materials in hand but the blessing that rested upon it."[2]

God even provides for us when we have *nothing* to offer! Once Peter unwisely engaged in dialogue with the local IRS about Jesus and potential charges of tax evasion. When the Savior gently reprimanded him, Peter had no rebuttal. Yet, with a single coin found in the mouth of the disciple's newly caught fish, Jesus paid not only His but also Peter's taxes (Matt. 17:24-27).

"Squeaky Voice"

I recently read about Antonio, a little Italian boy who couldn't sing in the school choir because of his very unpleasant-sounding voice. In fact, Antonio's friends called him "Squeaky Voice."[3]

Because the discouraged Antonio was equally deficient at learning to play a musical instrument, he spent most of his time whittling. Finally, Antonio's parents sent him to apprentice with a violin maker.

Though Antonio's story unfolded centuries ago, the violins he made, known today as Stradivarius violins, still sell for as much as $100,000 apiece!

Even when all we have to offer Christ is imbalance and hopelessness, He still wants that. He still desires to show us when to change and how. He still waits to help us "put on" what will bring better balance to our lives.

I can't tell you how many times I have to pray the following prayer:

"Dear Lord, Sometimes I feel like a juggler who is trying to keep too many balls in the air at once. Sometimes—too often, in fact—I lose control. Things start crashing around me, and I realize how helpless I am. Therefore, I'm here, again, asking You for help.

"Looking at the big picture, I realize the general areas in which I feel the most overwhelmed right now are _____ . I am desperate enough to make some changes if You will show me how.

"During this transition period from imbalance to better balance, I want to focus on this Bible verse/passage/promise as my 'theme text' during this time: _____ . It states, '_____ .'

"I praise You in advance, Lord, for steadying my feet on life's balance beam. I know Your plan for me is already in place, and I thank You. In the name of Your Son I pray. Amen."

Why a Theme Text?

Before finishing this chapter together, let's talk briefly about why one would want to select a theme text while working toward better balance.

Once again, we want to follow the example of Jesus.

In order to be victorious, Christ always "put on" the Word of God (Eph. 6:17). His response to Satan in the wilderness after that first near-overwhelming temptation was, "It is written, 'Man shall not live by bread alone, but *by every word that proceeds from the mouth of God*'" (Matt. 4:4, NKJV).

Christ demonstrated that God's Word must be the driving force behind our daily choices. This reality leads us to our third Better Balance Principle.

Better Balance Principle 3

Effective commitment to changing imbalance in my life will be based on God's Word (Matt. 4:4, 7, 10) or on urgings by the Holy Spirit that can be biblically supported (1 John 4:1).

As with Jesus in the upper room, we want to willingly "put on" (make changes) that which is in accordance with the revealed will of God. And only in God's Word, with the Holy Spirit "renewing" our minds, do we find His perfect will revealed (Rom. 12:1, 2).

A Quick Look at Your Notebook

Look again at your "Past Attempts at Balance" list from chapter 2 (or on the first page in your notebook, if that is where you wrote your responses).

Reread your past resolutions and commitments. Then underline only those for which your motive could be *Bible-based*. (By the way, the Bible would support your motive to be physically fit—through diet, weight control, and exercise—if it is in agreement with the principles of 3 John 2 or Galatians 5:23.)

Back to Interstate 5

Some of us may feel that making choices based on biblical principles would be taking too great a risk. After all, we might fail—again. Or worse, others viewing us as "professional" Christians might perceive us as failures when we don't live up to their expectations.

Didn't that big-rig driver in front of me on Interstate 5 take quite a risk? After all, he certainly opened himself up to public scrutiny by posting his "I'm a professional driver" notice on the back of the trailer. Besides simply inviting people's opinions, he also provided a telephone number!

Evidently the big-rig driver took these risks because he knew he had a track record of commendable conduct and was confident of his driving abilities.

When making choices based on Bible principles, we may not be confident in who we are (possibly because of our dismal track record?). However, we *can* be confident of who God is! His track record of standing behind the promises in His Word is flawless.

As Christ in the upper room "put on" that which was essential for knowing and doing His Father's will, He will also clothe us with what is needful for us to experience more peace and less stress.

Perhaps the apostle Paul best summed up this exchange of garments that we've been discussing.

"And do this, knowing the time, that now it is high time to awake out of sleep; for now our salvation is nearer than when we first believed. The night is far spent, the day is at hand. Therefore let us *cast off* the works of darkness, and let us put on the armor of light.

Let us walk properly" (Rom. 13:11-13, NKJV).

Paul ends this passage by pointing out the best Garment of all: "But put on the Lord Jesus Christ, and make no provision for the flesh, to fulfill its lusts" (verse 14).

HOMEWORK FOR THE HEART

"Dear Lord, please replace my faltering steps with the confidence that comes from putting on Your beauty of character and purity of motive. Thank You for hearing and answering my prayer. In Your name I pray. Amen."

Reminder: The best time to give our lives to God for the reclothing and balance of Bible principles is when our lives seem the most out of whack.

---

[1] E. C. McKenzie, *14,000 Quips and Quotes,* p. 78.

[2] Bob Laurent, *Watchman Nee, Man of Suffering* (Uhrichsville, Ohio: Barbour Books, 1998), p. 163.

[3] From *Cornerstone Connections Youth Resource Magazine,* first quarter 2002, pp. 36, 37.

CHAPTER 8

GABBING WITH THE GIRLS

HANGING ON UNTIL WE "GET IT"

*"Does your life seem to be out of control? Ask God for help.
He's done a great job with the universe."*[1]

"Nothing worthwhile ever happens in a hurry—so be patient!"
—Anonymous[2]

NOT ONLY DO WE WANT BETTER BALANCE changes in our lives to be Bible-based, but we also want to be certain they are appropriate within our unique context.

One afternoon, soon after our arrival in Africa for mission service, a couple of new African girlfriends dropped by for a visit—a visit I will *never* forget!

I offered my new friends seats in the living room. They sat opposite me and smiled. One looked me up and down and—completely out of the blue—said, "It's fine to do that when you're with us, but it's better not to do that when *men* are present."

"Do *what?*" I asked.

"Sit with your legs crossed," she answered.

"Why? What's wrong with that?" I asked.

She answered, "In our culture, only *men* have the privilege of crossing their legs in public. We women need to sit with both feet on the floor at all times."

After a pause, the other woman smiled at me and said, "It's all right to do that with your eyes when you're with *us,* but it's better not to do that when *men* are present."

"Not to do *what* with my eyes?" I asked.

"Look directly at men," she answered.

"So how am I *supposed* to look at them?" I asked.

"Well, you always avert your eyes or lower your gaze when speaking to a man or when men are coming in the opposite direction, like when you're on the way to the market."

"Oh, speaking of walking to the market," the first woman interrupted, "if you go cross-country instead of walking on the road, you'll come to a stream or two."

"That's no problem," I interrupted. "I'll just jump over them."

"Oh, *no!*" protested the second woman. "You must *never* jump over a stream. You have to *wade* across; you know—get your feet wet."

"But why?"

"Because jumping over streams is uniquely the privilege of men."

"Whew!" I pursed my lips and put my hand to my forehead.

"Oh, *please* remember not to do *that* when men are present!" they both implored.

"Not to do *what?*" I demanded, beginning to feel overwhelmed.

"Don't whistle," they said in unison, "because whistling is uniquely—"

"The privilege of men," I chimed in this time.

"Is there anything *else* I should know?"

The two women sat in merciful silence.

Just when I was about to let out a sigh of relief, one said to the other, "Mmm, maybe we should tell her about the trees and the roofs."

"Oh yeah—*that,*" nodded the other one.

"What about trees and roofs?" I asked.

The women smiled sympathetically, if not a bit condescendingly, at my transparent naïveté. Then one of them explained as if to a child. "As a woman you are not to climb trees or go up on roofs."

"Because . . . ?" I awaited the explanation.

"Because that would put you physically higher than men. And of course, being higher is one of those privileges reserved exclusively for the men."

Hypothetical Situation

About that time I began getting a bit hot under my Western-culture collar. I took a deep breath so as to keep my voice from rising. Choosing my words carefully, I asked, "Let me give you a hypothetical situation. Let's say that my little boy and I are home alone. He throws a toy up on the edge of the roof and it gets stuck up there, and I'm the only one home to get it down. Do you mean to tell me I can't get a little ladder and go up and get it?"

"That's right," the women nodded.

"Help me out here," I continued. "I'm still not understanding this. In my hypothetical situation, give me just one clear, *logical* reason that I should not get up on a ladder."

"All right," one of the women cheerfully and matter-of-factly answered. "If you did that, the men of the village might come over and beat you up."

"Oh!" I gasped as if someone had just thrown ice water in my face. "Oh, OK. *Now* I get it! OK—that's a *very* logical reason!"

At that point the discussion died a natural death, for I had no further questions. At least I had hung in there until I "got it."

Decisions, Decisions

In the mission field weeks and years that followed, I had some choices to make. The information—or decision-making "principles"—my new friends had shared with me made me more accountable than I would have been had I not known this information.

Therefore, my subsequent decisions, more often than not, involved choosing between my personal inclinations and doing the right thing in that culture's context.

When I honored my girlfriends' advice, I offended no one. However, when I did things my way (or *my* culture's way), responses ranged from raised eyebrows at one end of the scale to impaired ministry and hard feelings at the other.

In previous chapters we discussed three Better Balance principles to consider when making balance-enhancing changes in our lives. They involve

- the importance of making changes in the context of a love relationship with God;
- the importance of submitting our will to God's will;

- the importance of basing our changes on biblical principles.

(Note: The fourth and final Better Balance principle will be discussed in chapter 13.)

As with the "principles" my African girlfriends shared with me, the Better Balance principles will often lead us to decision crossroads where we must choose between doing our own thing or God's thing.

By the way, doing the latter is not as risky as you might think. "God does not design that our will should be destroyed, for it is only through its exercise that we can accomplish what He would have us do. Our will is to be yielded to Him, that we may receive it again, purified and refined, and so linked in sympathy with the Divine that He can pour through us the tides of His love and power."[3]

Wow! Every time I come to the end of this quote my spirit is overwhelmed. Imagine! God wants to so purify and refine our desires and so link them in sympathy with His that He can use *us* as vessels to bless others with His love and power!

That's why He bears so patiently with us. David promised that "the Lord is merciful and gracious, slow to anger, and plenteous in mercy. . . . He hath not dealt with us after our sins; nor rewarded us according to our iniquities" (Ps. 103:8-10).

God wants us to be joyful, balanced, fulfilled—helping others experience the same in Him!

In my living room that muggy afternoon in Africa, two new and loving friends patiently bore with me until I finally "got it." I am so grateful that they did!

Similarly, aren't you even more grateful that we have a loving heavenly Father who likewise patiently bears with us—over and over—until we finally "get it"?

I am!

HOMEWORK FOR THE HEART

Getting Personal. In chapter 6's "Areas in Which I Need God's Help to Change" section, you identified a *general* area (or two) in which you would like God's help for making some needed changes.

Brainstorm with yourself now and note any *specific* changes you need to make within those *general* areas.

"Dear Lord, You know better than I do that I need to make

these specific changes in my life: _____ ,

_____ , and _____ .

You also know how hard it is for me to put principled choices above
my own inclinations. Yet, like Peter trying to walk on the waves, I
am sinking! It's only a matter of time before I go under unless I reach
out anew to You.

"So, Jesus, right now I'm reaching for Your hand. Please help
me start making some very necessary changes. But most of all, help
me completely surrender all these things into the loving hands that
were nailed to the cross for me."

*Reminder: God will patiently bear with us as we continue to learn that
doing things in His ways results in greater strength, eventual happiness, and
better balance.*

---

[1] *God Speaks,* p. 55.
[2] E. C. McKenzie, *14,000 Quips and Quotes,* p. 384.
[3] Ellen G. White, *Thoughts From the Mount of Blessings,* p. 62.

▲

CHAPTER 9

"BUT IF NOT . . ."

ONE GIANT STEP BEYOND THE SHOCK COLLAR

"But if not, be it known unto thee, O king, that we will not serve thy gods,
nor worship the golden image which thou hast set up."
—*The three worthies to Nebuchadnezzar*★

BECAUSE SAM, OUR BLACK LAB-TYPE MIX, was lonely at Christmas that year, we went to the dog pound and got him a present—Jake. Jake was a chow mix with a perpetual "smile" on his face.

Since the two were both "outside dogs," as my late father would say, and shared the same kennel, they became inseparable. So they took turns guarding, tussling, barking, chasing balls, and digging gopher holes.

First, the sleek Sam would dig down to his "elbows" in a potentially promising gopher hole. Then the more stoutly built Jake would muscle in for some excavation action. Jake's broad shoulders and powerful front legs would churn in a yellow furry blur until his tongue hung out the side of his mouth.

The waiting Sam would see his next opportunity and pounce his ready paws into the growing cavity, preempting Jake. Dirt would fly as even his head disappeared into the cavern deepened by this renewed digging frenzy.

How Jim and I would laugh, especially when holes got big enough for both dogs to simultaneously dig. Eventually only their tail ends were still above ground.

We didn't laugh, however, when we watched Sam's sleek rear end—followed by Jake's bronze hindquarters—disappearing down

the road. Dog owners, in exasperated tones, refer to this phe-
nomenon as "running away."

Sam had always been a well-mannered and even a well-trained
dog. He was obedient and submissive until he acquired this annoy-
ing habit from an undisciplined neighbor dog.

Now, unless Jim and I were extremely vigilant on walks with the
dogs, Sam would sniff a passing animal scent and be gone—no matter how loudly we pleaded, sweet-talked, or yelled. Jake soon followed Sam's lead. Sometimes the two dogs would be gone for two
or three days at a time.

Extremely annoyed, my husband would have to leave his urgent
farm tasks, crawl up into the pickup truck, and go in search of them.
With a sense of shame, I'd get on the telephone and alert the neighbors—once again—to be on the lookout for two friendly dogs on
the lam.

Hot-Dog Heaven

Once Sam and Jake took off on a Friday afternoon. The following Monday morning a friendly-sounding woman phoned us. "Are
you missing a big black dog and a big fluffy yellow one?" she inquired.

"Yes, we are," admitted my husband.

"Well, they're here and are the sweetest things. In fact, they've
spent the entire weekend here in the house with us."

"In your *house?*"

"Yes, and my husband just fell for them. He's made several trips
to town so they'd have enough hot dogs to eat."

"Hot dogs!" exclaimed Jim incredulously.

"They just love them," she chuckled. "The black dog spent his
nights in the big recliner. The yellow dog seemed to prefer the fluffy
throw rug in front of the chair. If we had more room in our little
mobile home, we'd sure like to keep them!"

Shock Collar

"That does it!" said Jim, putting down the phone. "We can't have
our dogs running around the country like this, imposing on people—
eating their hot dogs! I hate to do this, but after I get them home, I'm

going to have to get out the shock collar to use on our walks."

Prior to our next walk with the dogs, Jim reluctantly put the shock collar on Sam and took him for a walk. When Sam started running off, Jim punched the button of the remote control. Sam emitted a quick yap as a sudden surge of electricity stung his neck. He came running back.

Then Jim put the shock collar on Jake and pushed the button when Jake started running away. Jake responded in a similar manner.

"I don't know what to do," said Jim. "We have two dogs and only one shock collar. Seems like a waste of money to get another collar when they're so expensive." He walked in silence for a moment. "Say, maybe I could make a counterfeit shock collar!"

And he did. The real collar consisted of a small but weighty electronic receiver box attached to the throat side of a heavy collar. My ingenious husband fashioned the counterfeit collar by attaching a similar-shaped block of wood to an extra collar. To make it approximately the same weight as the electronic receiver box on the real collar, he screwed a large fishing weight to the wooden block.

Whenever we took the dogs walking after that, each dog "thought" he was wearing the shock collar, although only one of them had the real thing around his neck.

When Sam would start to run away and Jim activated a quick shock, Sam would yelp and run back to us. Amazingly, Jake would also yelp and hurry back to us as well. On days when Jake had to be briefly "jolted" back into the world of good behavior, Sam would respond as if he too had been shocked.

In a short amount of time the dogs began learning from each other's mistakes and rarely tried running off anymore.

Not Learning From the Mistakes of Others

When reading the Bible in my earlier Christian experience, I often wondered why it didn't contain more narratives about truly balanced people whose stories had happy endings. Why so many stories about unbalanced individuals who made choices that ruined their lives?

As time passed, however, I started realizing the divine wisdom behind the inclusion of these particularly painful tales. God had put a "shock collar" on Cain and Samson and even David to help me avoid making similar mistakes.

Often, how the main character responded to these "jolts" determined the quality of their life, not to mention their eternal destiny.

Let's look briefly at three Bible characters and how they relay to us some helpful secondhand wake-up jolts.

Judas Iscariot spent three and a half years of his life—the final three and a half years—trudging around Galilee at the side of Jesus. During this period he observed, firsthand, the havoc sinful choices wreaked in the lives of those who came (or were brought) to Christ. Judas came into contact with tightfisted tax collectors and loose women.

He observed, face to face, the horrifying condition of those who had given Satan so much ground that demons now inhabited their minds and bodies.

From Christ's own lips Judas heard pronouncements of damnation against pharisaical pride, selfishness, and greedy ambition. He noted Christ's sorrow when the rich young ruler chose wealth and position over the kingdom of God. Each unbalanced person Judas encountered was a divine jolt from Heaven's shock collar. Each observation of sin's painful consequences was a wake-up call for him to surrender his self-ambitious agenda to the will of God.

In the upper room Judas, with deeply mixed emotions, looked at the top of his Master's head bending before him. He felt the Savior pour cool water over his dusty feet. Judas, knowing his own heart to be that of a would-be traitor, keenly felt a sudden thrill of love pulse through his being. Maybe Christ knew best, after all. Even yet, it was not too late to break his deal with the high priest.

Moments later at the Communion table Jesus offered Judas bread and wine. Once again an electrical tension squeezed the deceitful disciple's heart. Though Judas well remembered his appointment with the high priest—within the hour even—he could still refuse the silver-coined payoff for helping set up an imminent nocturnal ambush. So why not just reveal everything to the compassionate Jesus right now and let Him deal with the mess?

Perhaps he rationalized, *Am I not going to bring balance to the Jewish nation by forcing Christ's hand to declare Himself king? Then He can mobilize us to throw off this yoke of Roman oppression, and I'll get the credit for making it happen.*

Instead of responding to the reality checks Christ so graciously provided, Judas went through with his plans. What tragic results! Within a few hours he died by his own hand (Matt. 26:14-16; 27:4-10).

Learning From Others

Shadrach, Meshach, and Abednego, on the other hand, were well aware that their nation was experiencing a Babylonian captivity because of disobedience-caused imbalance. For centuries Jehovah had graciously borne with His chosen people who were living outside of His choosing—outside of the covenant He had made with them.

The three young Hebrews had heard many stories while growing up. Each story fell into one of two categories: when Israel obeyed God, He abundantly blessed them. When they disobeyed God, He silently withdrew from them. After all, that *had* been the original covenant God had made with His chosen people (see chapters 27-33 of Deuteronomy).

The three worthies chose to learn from the mistakes of others. When Babylonian king Nebuchadnezzar himself pressured the young men to disobey their God by worshiping the giant image on the plain of Dura, they remembered the shock collar (Ex. 20:3-6) and refused to do so.

They not only surrendered their wills to God, but they went a step beyond surrender. They *committed* to doing God's will no matter what the consequences.

When Nebuchadnezzar cautioned Shadrach, Meshach, and Abednego that their commitment to God might result in their being consumed in his fiery furnace, the three young men assured the king they served a God who could deliver them.

They added, "But if not . . ." (Dan. 3:18).

Though they didn't know the outcome of their commitment, they knew that God would be with them. And He was! In fact, God's own Son was waiting to embrace and sustain them—in the very heart of the fiery ordeal!

The Unlikely Man of God's Own Heart

Most of us are not as crafty and dark-minded as Judas. Neither are we as wholesome and single-minded as the three worthies. We fall somewhere in between these two extremes. Sort of like David did.

Thank God for David's shock collar story in the Bible!

At some level or other, we can probably see bits of ourselves in David's moral fall with Bathsheba and his subsequent murder of her husband. Like David, we too want our own way because it temporarily "feels good." We too are very clever at rationalizing why we should get it. We too cause hurt and pain when we try to cover up one mistake with another and then another.

Yet, like David, we too can change direction when Heaven's "shock collar" jolts us back to spiritual reality (2 Sam. 12:13). In David's case the prophet Nathan administered the shock. Though David's choices had "given great occasion to the enemies of the Lord to blaspheme" (verse 14), David was ever ready to admit, and surrender, his sinful past to God. As soon as he made this decision, notice how quickly God forgave him. In the next breath the prophet reveals to David, "The Lord also hath put away thy sin; thou shalt not die" (verse 13). What a loving relationship David had with his God!

David understood that he could make balanced choices only when God was at work in his life. Whoever wrote Psalm 119 knew the necessity of meditating on God and His words. Choices start in the mind. Where the mind leads, actions follow.

In David's famous psalm regarding that dark episode in his life (Psalm 51), he not only surrendered his will to God's but he also made a permanent commitment. He promised God that from that time forward he would teach "transgressors thy ways" so that sinners would be brought to God (Ps. 51:13). In other words, the grim consequences of David's choices would "shock" others away from making similar ones.

Moreover, I find so amazing God's final assessment of David: "A man after My own heart." Evidently David's renewed commitment was a step deeper into the heart of God.

Christ and Commitment

Commitment was important not only to David but also to Jesus. For, as with us, He called His earlier disciples to a "but if not . . ." commitment. Church tradition suggests that the majority of the 12 original apostles lived out their commitment to a martyr's end.

Do you recall, however, that in addition to the disciples whom Jesus called, a number of other individuals also *asked* to be close followers of His? Yet some of these individuals put *limitations* on their surrender (Luke 9:57-61). They told Christ that before they could be truly committed, they had places to go and people to see. Unlike the three worthies, they were not willing to take a stand for "but if not . . ."

Christ's response to their lukewarm, commitment-less lip service was "I want *all* of you" (see Matt. 19:29). I want the same wholehearted *forever* commitment of love from you that you can expect from Me (see Luke 9:62).

End-Time Would-be Disciples

Christ tells end-time would-be disciples, us, the same (Rev. 3:14-22). What will be our choices? Like Sam and Jake, will we choose to learn the lesson of the shock collar? Will we surrender *all* the imbalance-causing details in our lives to Christ?

If we are willing to learn from others' experiences, we are also willing to go one step beyond surrender.

We are willing to *commit*—to surrender every aspect of our lives to a growing love relationship with Jesus and to ever-increasing balance.

Yes, a total commitment may one day lead to a fiery furnace. Yet it will also lead us to the unshakable conviction that already walking in persecution's flames is our faithful God—the God of "but if not . . ."

HOMEWORK FOR THE HEART

Wholehearted Commitment. What first-time or renewed commitment would you like to make to God?

Note: In terms of balanced day-to-day living, our having a personal mission statement (or statement of purpose, as some people refer to it) may help keep the whats and whys and hows of our commitment before us.

In the following chapter we'll briefly look at 10 ways in which Christ maintained perfect balance in His life.

Reminder: Learning from the mistakes of out-of-balance people in the past can save us from making many of our own.

★ Dan. 3:18.

▲

CHAPTER 10

THE MASTER RAFTER

HOW JESUS STAYED VERTICAL

"Be perfect, therefore, as your heavenly Father is perfect."
—Matt. 5:48, NIV

THE LITTLE SCALY PATCH, with its field of underlying red, lay flush against the skin on my left forearm.

It's probably just a scratch that got infected a bit, I thought. I applied some skin lotion formulated for "extra-dry skin" and assumed I'd taken care of the problem.

Two weeks later the scaly patch was still there. By now a deep itch identified the spot so pointedly that I could have applied lotion in the dark. *It's probably some long-lasting poison oak I picked up down in the grove,* I decided. Once again, while rifling through the bathroom cupboard for anti-itch ointment, I confidently sensed I was taking care of the problem.

Two weeks later a local pharmacist counseled, "You might try an over-the-counter hydrocortisone cream. That should clear up the inflammation."

Seven dollars' worth of cream and six weeks later, the circumference of the red scaly spot on my arm was continuing to grow. Suddenly I realized I really had no control over this worrisome blight on my skin whose irritation had progressed beyond skin-deep. I visited my doctor.

He took one look at it and, like an old acquaintance, called it by name—some nine-syllable medical term I couldn't pronounce.

What I *do* remember, however, is his layperson's explanation of that term: "At this spot you have the definite beginnings of skin cancer. This is not going to go away."

However, his next pronouncement flooded my mind with relief. "I can remove this from your arm in about 45 seconds." And with some type of painful freezing process, he did.

The Great Physician

Jesus Christ is the only one who can excise growing imbalance from our lives and replace it with His healthy balance. As with my applying various lotions, you and I alone can't help ourselves. We don't know how to eradicate the *source* of the problem.

Before Jesus died a perfect death, He also lived in perfect balance on this earth. With a sense of peace He stayed vertical despite any craziness coming His direction.

Let's look at 10 coping techniques Christ demonstrated in order to balance perfectly the stresses of His life.

1. Christ balanced people time with solitary time in the presence of His heavenly Father. (In order to do this, Jesus had to set boundaries. See Luke 4:42, 43 for one of these boundary-setting times.) A river rafter might refer to this technique as "putting on a life jacket."

Less than two miles from our house runs a stretch of southern Oregon's Rogue River. The river's long, winding channel attracts hundreds of river rafters every summer. Most rafting trips end happily. Yet, from time to time, a raft or an inner tube explodes when coming in contact with sharp rocks in shallow channels.

Sometime back an experienced rafter drowned during a rafting trip when he fell from his raft just as it passed over white-water rapids. His frantic rafting buddies last saw him as his wet head disappeared beneath the swirling foam.

The following day search-and-rescue workers discovered the rafter's body washed up on the shore several miles below the point from where he'd been thrown into the river. Investigators later surmised that a strong undertow had sucked him into a vortex, holding him there until a stronger current tugged him out and carried him downriver.

When rescuers discovered the body they immediately noticed one detail about the drowning victim: he had *not* been wearing a life jacket, which could have saved his life.

At the school where I taught, located only a few miles from the Rogue River, the older students looked forward each spring to the annual rafting trip. Some of the more self-confident students balked at the inconvenience of having to wear a dank-smelling life jacket. Not only was it bulky but it also interfered with the perfect tan they hoped to absorb that day.

We teachers had to remind our students about fatal rafting incidents similar to the one I just related. Of course, the kids would eventually agree that the extra measure of safety was well worth the bother of wearing a life jacket.

Likewise, taking time with God each day may seem bothersome at the start of our obligation-filled mornings. Yet doing so enables Him to clothe us with a spiritual life jacket before we launch out into the stress-laden rapids and hidden temptation undertows of our days.

As with a rafter's life jacket, our spiritual protection may mean the difference between life and death. Jesus knew this and, therefore, took time each day to put on His Father's life jacket by spending time with Him.

2. Christ balanced the emotional drain of daily stress with physical refreshment breaks. He arranged short getaways for Himself—whether it was to a fishing boat on Lake Galilee or a hike up a nearby mountain.

Like Christ, we need to balance our daily reality with occasional mini-getaways—even if they're nothing more than a regular morning walk, a few minutes with an old guitar, or a pick-up-and-put-down hobby such as scrapbooking.

3. Christ balanced the negativity and misery around Him by filling His mind with the positive, the true, the uplifting. "Nothing tends more to promote health of body and of soul than does a spirit of gratitude and praise. It is a positive duty to resist melancholy, discontented thoughts and feelings—as much a duty as it is to pray."[1]

My mother had been dealing with the loss of my father. They were married 63 years. While I was visiting with her one afternoon, she admitted, "I'm really down today. I've been trying to figure out why I've had this sudden feeling of heaviness."

We talked about what it felt like and when it had started. Suddenly she commented, "Do you know what? I think my depression started yesterday afternoon while I was listening to a talk show that was a real downer. Everybody on the show was talking about how personal loss was ruining their lives. It was after listening to all of them that my own thoughts started taking a nosedive."

I doubt that Jesus would find too much positive and uplifting in most of today's media. Several people have told me they have started to limit the amount of television news that they watch, because too much negative information affects them emotionally.

Some people read self-help books for encouragement. Many of these books provide excellent counsel and help. Others, however, are quietly infused with pantheism, New Age philosophies, self-worship, and encouragement to live ungodly lifestyles.

More than one author of self-help books has implied, if not openly stated, that God is none other than our true selves.

When reading positive, self-help matter, let's still be *biblically* discerning about the purity of our sources.

4. *Jesus balanced time spent with needy people by spending time with nurturing people.* Sometimes compassionate, empathetic individuals find that the majority of their friends are becoming ones who drain them emotionally. How wonderful to be there for others! Yet we need to balance needy friendships with those that nurture us, as well.

5. *Christ balanced work time with social time.* The Bible tells us Jesus took short camping trips with His disciples. He also took time out to go to weddings and dinner parties. He used these social opportunities to find out more about people's lives and interests so that He could better minister to them later on.[2]

6. *Our Lord balanced preaching time (mental exercise) with outdoor time (physical exercise, fresh air, and sunshine).* What is your personal physical exercise program? Do you and I need to make some changes in our daily schedule to allow for a better one?

7. *Jesus balanced the frenzied lives around Him by maintaining a simple lifestyle.* What aspects of our lives can you and I simplify?

8. *Our Savior coped by often delegating responsibilities to others.* Maybe

we need to delegate more to our children, spouses, church coworkers, relatives, or colleagues.

9. Jesus coped with the hopelessness of the present life by keeping a constant focus on a better future life. At all times Jesus kept before Himself the reality that this world was not His home. He reminded His followers that it wasn't theirs either (John 14:1-3). His choices and lifestyle reflected His strong belief that, sooner or later, He was going home. Do ours?

10. Christ denied self-pitying thoughts and actions by reserving His sympathies for the uplifting of others. From the manger to the grave "the Son of man came not to be ministered unto, but to minister" (Mark 10:45). He calls us to imitate His example. "Take my yoke upon you" (Matt. 11:29).

This text, however, doesn't end with this command—it ends with a promise: "And ye shall find rest" (verse 29). What wonderful news for the overstressed trying to stay vertical on life's balance beam!

"In the Saviour's invitation the promise of rest is united with the call to labor. . . . The heart that rests most fully upon Christ will be most earnest and active in labor for Him"[3]

Proverbs 11:25 tells us that "he who refreshes others will himself be refreshed" (NIV).

How grateful I am to the authors of the four Gospels for recording so much of Christ's life. His words and actions show us that we can share God's love wherever we are! When it comes right down to it, *no one* has the exact same sphere of influence that *you* do—the exact same family members, the exact same levels of friendships with the exact same people. *No one* else can tell others *your* story of God's goodness in your life exactly like you can.

As I couldn't fix my skin problem without the doctor's help, neither can we maintain balance without God's help. When we allow the Master Rafter to clothe us in His life jacket, we will stay afloat while navigating each day's raging rapids and hidden undertows. His coping-with-stress techniques will become second nature to us. If anyone knows about rapids and undertows, it's Jesus.

Remember: He's the one who walked *on* water!

HOMEWORK FOR THE HEART

Your Balancing Act. Skim over Christ's 10 balancers (in italic print). Now take a bird's-eye view of your personal daily/weekly schedule. Prioritize the 10 balancers discussed in this chapter and list them in the following order: let number one on your list be the balancer you have been neglecting most. List as number two your second-most neglected balancer, and so on.

When you finish, ask God to show you one change to make concerning number one (only!) on your list. (You may want to concentrate on the others later—don't overwhelm yourself with too much change at once). Work out the details within the context of your daily schedule, and make a commitment to God about this item.

Finally, phone a friend who cares about you (someone who won't get on your case if you should blow it but who will commit to praying for you). Tell him or her about your commitment and ask that you be held accountable.

Reminder: Christ's lifestyle reveals principles by which we can cope with the major stressors in our lives.

---

[1] Ellen G. White, *The Ministry of Healing,* p. 251.

[2] *Ibid.,* pp. 17-28.

[3] White, *Steps to Christ,* p. 71.

CHAPTER 11

▲

DUDE, WHY ARE YOU RUNNING?

LIVING WITH PURPOSE

"A sense of mission gives meaning and significance to our lives."
—*Dr. Ron Jenson*

"My food is to do the will of Him who sent Me, and to finish His work."
—*Jesus Christ*[1]

WHEN GYMNASTS WALK ON THE BALANCE BEAM, they must have a clear concept not only of their destination but also of what they plan to do in the meantime—like Messenger A in the following story.

Centuries ago a king sent an army to fight his nation's archenemy. The army commander sent a runner with an update, knowing that the king back in his palace anxiously awaited news from the front lines. We'll call the runner Messenger A.

Just after Messenger A took off down a road leading to the capital city, another soldier rushed up to the commander. In a state of excitement, he made a passionate request: "Let me run too!"

"Why?" the commander asked. "You don't have a reason to run—I've given you no updates."

"I don't care—just let me run!" the soldier pleaded.

"Well, run then!" the commander conceded.

Self-appointed Messenger B disappeared down the road in a cloud of dust.

Sometime later, a watchman on the palace wall called down to the king, who was sitting near the city's main gate. "Your Majesty, I see someone running. . . . Oh, wait a minute! I see someone else behind him."

Somehow Messenger B had overtaken and passed Messenger A.

Rushing inside the city gates, Messenger B bowed low before the king.

"Your Majesty," he said, struggling to catch his breath, "all is well."

"What do you mean by that?" asked the king. "And what about my son—did he get killed in the fighting or is he still alive?"

"Hmm," mused the messenger. "You know, I'm not really too sure."

I imagine that everyone within earshot felt betrayed by the messenger with no report. The watchman on the wall probably felt like calling down, "Dude, if you don't know anything, why are you running?"

Messenger B stumbled over his next words. "Well, uh, I saw a lot of confusion on the battlefield and—"

"Step aside!" ordered the king to the messenger who had run without a purpose.

Just then Messenger A ran through the city gates and straight to the king. He too bowed low. Then he related to the king *exactly* what had transpired on the battlefield.[2]

Defining the Purpose of Our "Run"

Perhaps some of us are *still* confused about which changes to make in our lives in order to experience better balance. Perhaps that's because we are trying to "run" without a clear purpose in mind.

As author William Covey notes, "trying to prioritize activities before you even know how they relate to your sense of personal mission and how they fit into the balance of your life is not effective. You may be prioritizing and accomplishing things you don't want or need to be doing at all."[3]

In recent years a vast number of individuals wanting to achieve better balance—whether in the Christian world or business world—have developed their own personal mission statements. In fact, one can now purchase entire books whose main purpose is to help the reader draft a personal mission statement.

A clearly defined mission statement facilitates our running with purpose in the following ways.

- *A personal mission statement helps us prioritize our limited time, energy, and resources so that God's revealed purpose for our lives isn't buried—along with us—beneath a crushing load of items from other people's agendas.*

Most of us don't have a problem with saying yes. We do have a problem, however, with saying no. Of course, we want to be there for other people and their needs—but in God's ways and in God's timing.

- *A personal mission statement simplifies our decision-making by enabling us to prioritize the competing components of our daily lives.*

Author Julie-Allyson Ieron writes: "Whatever we determine to be our life's guiding objective will become the yardstick by which we measure everything in our daily agendas, every thought we entertain, every word we say, every action we undertake."[4]

A friend of ours recently confided, "If an activity or choice or purchase (as harmless as it may be) doesn't specifically fit into the purpose for either our marriage or our personal walks with Christ, we just don't do it."

What can you eliminate in your life that doesn't fit into your purpose: certain TV shows, magazines, irrelevant e-mail forwards, purposeless obligations and activities, or even certain food items?

- *A mission statement strengthens us in setting personal boundaries.* I used to struggle with not being able to say no to anyone who asked for any favor, and I was often overwhelmed. Since I'm now living with a personal mission statement, I find it much easier to set boundaries on my time and energy resources.
- *A personal mission statement provides us a sense of security.* Even when I fail to make good on my good intentions, my mission statement reminds me that my *goals* are still in place and that tomorrow is yet another day filled with new opportunities to "get it right."
- *Finally, a personal mission statement holds us accountable.* It holds us accountable for who our role models are. It holds us accountable for what we look at or think about when we're alone. It holds us accountable for how we spend our extra money and our extra time. What we're doing with our minds and with our time right now will come back either to haunt or help us when the chips are down.

Ask yourself this: "The next time a terrorist attack or earthquake or sudden personal loss threatens to throw me into a state of near panic, what do I want to come flashing into my mind so that my response will be balanced? A snatch of lyric or advertising jingle I've had ingrained from years of mindless radio listening? Or snatches of Bible promises I've taken the time to memorize?" Verses such as:

- Proverbs 29:25: "Fear of man will prove to be a snare, but whoever trusts in the Lord is kept safe" (NIV).
- Matthew 24:6: "You will hear of wars and rumors of wars, but see to it that you are not alarmed. Such things must happen" (NIV).
- Luke 21:28: "When these things begin to take place, stand up and lift up your heads, because your redemption is drawing near" (NIV).
- The reassuring promises of Psalms 23 and 91 in the light of current world events![5]

Mission Statements That Made a Difference

A number of individuals in the Bible had clear-cut mission statements and "ran" with purpose, never looking back. Let's consider just a handful of these individuals and their purposes.

Esther: Even though she risked death in order to be true to her mission statement, Esther's choice (to be the best queen she could "for such a time as this") saved her nation (Esther 4:14, 16).

Paul: When he came to fully understand his purpose, Paul's choices took the gospel to the Gentiles: "To me, who am less than the least of all the saints, this grace was given, that I should preach among the Gentiles the unsearchable riches of Christ" (Eph. 3:8, NKJV).

Jesus: From an early age, Jesus demonstrated a strong sense of purpose (though the wording changed through the years, as yours might). At the age of 12 He stated to Joseph and Mary His purpose in the form of a question. "Did you not know that I must be about My Father's business?" (Luke 2:49, NKJV). Almost 20 years later His personal mission statement took this form: "My food is to do the will of Him who sent Me, and to finish His work" (John 4:34, NKJV), which was to rescue you and me—eternally—from the power and presence of sin.

Why not seriously consider prayerfully drafting a personal mission statement for this stage of your life journey?

Then, like Esther, you will have the *courage* to do what you must.

Like Paul, you will be able to "run with *patience*" (Heb. 12:1).

Like Messenger A, you will run with *purpose* in an off-kilter world.

And finally, like Jesus, you will also *run the risk* of making a profound difference in the lives of others.

HOMEWORK FOR THE HEART
Drafting My Mission Statement.

a. First review the items about yourself that you noted in chapter 5.

b. Then complete this statement, adding more sentences, if necessary.

"I sense that, at this season of life, my purpose is to _____

_____

_____

_____ ."

c. Supporting Bible passage(s) for my personal mission statement: _____

_____

_____ .

Reminder: Having a personal mission statement can help us define a purpose for the changes and choices we make.

[1] John 4:34, NKJV.

[2] See 2 Sam. 18:19-33.

[3] Stephen R. Covey, *The Seven Habits of Highly Effective People* (New York: Simon and Schuster, 1989), pp. 165-168.

[4] Julie-Allyson Ieron, *Believer's Life System,* women's ed. (Chicago: Moody Press, 1998); pages were unnumbered.

[5] Several people have shared with me that a nearly effortless way to brush up on what they believe (and why) is to take advantage of evangelistic series or prophecy seminars going on in their areas.

CHAPTER 12

▲

DETAILS, DETAILS!

IMPLEMENTING YOUR MISSION STATEMENT

"There are four steps to accomplishment:
Plan purposefully.
Prepare prayerfully.
Proceed positively.
Pursue persistently."★

I HOPE YOU HAVE AT LEAST A FIRST DRAFT of your personal mission statement. Maybe you are wondering how to go about implementing it.

Well, guess what? The "formula" isn't the same for everyone. In fact, based on the experiences of people in the Bible, I suspect that no two implementation "formulas" are exactly alike. No two people are exactly alike. No two sets of personal needs are exactly alike.

Please don't think, *But* my *situation is beyond help!* God once remarked to Sarah, "Is anything too hard for the Lord?" No situation of imbalance is ever beyond the healing power of Jesus.

The reason I venture this statement is because of what happened at the Pool of Bethesda (John 5:1-15). Few other stories in the Bible offer me greater reassurance, comfort, and encouragement. That's because the person in the story, a nameless paralytic, was worse off than I have ever been! The paralytic not only had difficulty moving forward on life's balance beam, but had apparently fallen off a long time before.

In fact, he had spent his days (the previous 38 years, actually) wasting away beside the pool at Bethesda's low-class health resort.

Loneliness and pain overwhelmed him. Remorse for past choices haunted him.

The selfishness of others surrounded him. The reality of his purposeless situation had bound him in chains of despair.

Then Jesus Came

Then Jesus came looking for him, as He comes in search of any of us who can no longer help ourselves.

However, the paralytic was so consumed by life gone awry that he didn't even recognize the Savior. So disorienting was his emotional and physical tailspin that he couldn't even give Jesus a straight answer to the Master's simple question: "Do you *want* to be healed?" All the sick man could do was weakly list reasons that healing, in his case, could never be an option.

Yet here, for me, is the energizing core of this story—Jesus healed him anyway!

Scripture tells us (verse 13) that this man didn't even *know* who Jesus was! Yet Jesus healed him! Christ's actions showed that He not only understood the paralytic's heart, He also understood his circumstances.

Our Circumstances

If Jesus could bring wholeness to a depressed, emotionally imbalanced, poverty-stricken, friendless paraplegic, what can't He do for you and me?

Your present circumstances may have you feeling like a slave to a toddler whose needs don't give you the time for solitude that you may so desperately crave.

Your circumstances may be an unexpected divorce sapping your emotional energy.

Your circumstances may be an ongoing health problem or an eating disorder.

Your circumstances may be the aftermath of unfair, cruel acts perpetrated against you when you were young, helpless, or naive.

Your circumstances may be the results of your own sinful choices.

Yet, dear friend of God and future joint heir with Christ, Jesus understands *your* circumstances. Even more important, Jesus understands your heart.

The heart He died to save.

The heart He longs to comfort.

The heart He so desperately wants you to give to Him, fragmented and out-of-balance though it may be.

When we give Jesus our hearts, we also give Him our love, our trust, our affections, our will. In short, we give Him our permission to go to work in our lives. In return, He gives us His peace, His wisdom, His comfort, and His grace-enabled power to make balance-enhancing choices.

Jesus didn't ask the paralytic to be instantaneously perfect. What He *did* ask him, though, was to get up on his feet and to take that *first step* toward a more joyful, productive life. Jesus will do the same for you and for me.

First Steps

Various domains comprise our daily lives: the spiritual, the emotional, the mental, the social, and the physical. Keeping each of these domains in balance with the others is challenging. One of these domains being out of balance seriously impacts the others. The state of the spiritual domain, for example, directly affects everything else in our lives.

When my son Kent was 11 years of age, he came home from a Christian summer camp with a new purpose: "I want to put God first." He made a commitment to spend at least 15 minutes a day reading his Bible and other devotional materials.

Though happy for his decision, I wondered how it would impact his homework preparation time. He had a terrible struggle with schoolwork, as he suffered from a mild learning disability.

Kent was faithful with his morning devotional commitment. With eventual remediation he was able to raise his grades from low Cs and Ds to a B–/C average by the time he became a junior at a private boarding school.

One day Kent phoned home with exciting news. "Mom, the academic decathlon coach has invited me to be on the school's decathlon team next year! He said he liked solid C students on it as well as A and B students. I'm going to pray about this."

I congratulated him but worried. "Lord," I prayed, "there's no way he can do this—not with his heavy class load and learning disability."

Kent decided to accept the decathlon coach's invitation against my better judgment. Since I feared his probable decathlon failure, I began negotiating with God.

"Lord, I know most of the decathlon competitors go away from this yearly competition without even one medal. I know there just aren't enough to go around. But Lord, You know how this child has put You first for years—against huge odds. *Please* honor his commitment to You. I'm not asking for the impossible. No gold. No silver. Just *one* of those dull bronze medals."

I prayed this prayer for a year—until the day the Santa Cruz County Academic Decathlon took place. That morning I awakened with a heavy dread in my heart. All day I pleaded, "God, please, just one *bronze* medal."

Parents were allowed to be present at the final Knowledge Bowl in the afternoon and then at the awards banquet in the evening.

As I sat with other moms, dads, and teachers from area schools at the evening banquet, I strongly suspected my "one little *bronze* medal" prayer had been asking too much.

I made small talk with Kent and his teammates until the end of the meal when the judges stepped up to the podium to present the awards.

One judge announced the academic category, another the name of each winner, while a third judge hung the earned medals around the necks of the winners.

Gamely I applauded the students called forward for recognition.

Suddenly one of the emcees announced, "And the *bronze* medal for *science* goes to . . . Kent Rathbun from Monterey Bay Academy." Kent's coach and teammates jumped to their feet cheering.

Through grateful tears, I watched the awarding judge hang *God's* bronze medal around the neck of my son.

Kent returned to our table, eyes sparkling. Face flushed, he slid into the chair beside me and opened his mouth to say something. Before he could get it out, the announcing judge declared, "Kent Rathbun of Monterey Bay Academy for the *silver* medal in literature!" Stunned, Kent made his way toward the podium while I struggled to my feet, applauding.

In Psalm 91:14, 15 God promises to honor openly those who have loved Him no matter the circumstances.

Before the awards ceremony ended, I watched God publicly honor a kid who had taken one simple step toward implementing his mission statement: to put God first in his life. By the end of the evening the judges had summoned Kent to the podium six times to receive three gold medals, two silver medals, and one bronze medal—the one for which I'd prayed.

Often, when we ask God to help us get our lives in balance, He begins to answer our prayer by working with us in the *spiritual* domain, as He did with my son. However, He may choose to work first in the *physical* domain—as He did with the paralytic beside the Pool of Bethesda.

According to our individual needs, He works with us out of infinite wisdom. The God who knows our circumstances, who understands our hearts, and who identifies with our unique challenges *always* stands ready to empower our first steps toward enhanced balance.

How exciting it will be to see where those first steps lead you as you begin to implement your mission statement!

HOMEWORK FOR THE HEART

Taking Some First Steps. The items in this section are simply ways of getting to know Christ better.

My Commitment(s) in the Spiritual Domain

Amount of time I will allot each day for:

- meditation and prayer (e.g., intercessory, journaling)

  _____

- Bible study (Bible books, topics, characters)

  _____

- Scripture memorization, starting with _____

_____(text)_____

- Doctrines, spiritual issues, beliefs I plan to research so that I

   can know exactly what I believe, and why _____

   _____

The exact times I plan to meet God:

Sunday _____ Monday _____

Tuesday _____ Wednesday _____

Thursday _____ Friday _____

Saturday _____

My Commitment(s) in the Emotional Domain
(me-time; healthy relationships)

1. _____

2. _____

3. _____

My Commitment(s) in the Physical Domain
(personal health, exercise, diet, lifestyle)

1. _____

2. _____

3. _____

My Commitment in the Mental Domain
(positive mental stimulation, memorization)

1. _____

2. _____

3. _____

My Commitment in the Social Domain
(interaction with others, personal morality, service)

1. _____

2. _____

3. _____

Amount of time I will allot each week (or month) to serve

others _____ .

Ways I can do this by myself include _____

_____ .

Ways I can accomplish this through my church programs in-

clude _____ .

Reminder: God doesn't ask us to commit to instantaneous perfection, but He does ask us to commit to prayerful, focused, grace-enabled growth.

_____
★ E. C. McKenzie, *14,000 Quips and Quotes*, p. 420.

CHAPTER 13

▲

THE CALEB CRISIS

BETTER BALANCE PRINCIPLE 4

"Love is an unusual game.
There are either two winners or none."★

ONE SUMMER I SERVED AS ASSISTANT DIRECTOR of a Christian young people's camp. Among the 150-plus campers whom the big yellow buses spilled out by the flagpole one week was a 9-year-old boy whom I will call Caleb.

Having lived in the same community with this child's family several years earlier, I already knew too much about them. For example, I knew an adult family member was serving time for domestic violence.

I also knew Caleb's mother was so financially destitute that she sometimes just camped in a park during summer months because she couldn't pay apartment rent. I knew the family obtained their food from a government assistance program—as well as from potlucks at a couple churches in the area.

Life's cruel injustices had already left little Caleb deeply scarred, extremely angry, and apparently emotionally troubled.

The first few days of camp Caleb—though small and skinny—had terrorized the other children. Even the adult staff members soon regarded him as a menace.

Midweek the camp secretary beeped my walkie-talkie. "Come to the office immediately," she said in terse tones. "We've got a big problem on our hands!"

At the office I found Caleb's angry counselor, firmly holding the boy by an upper arm. Caleb was wearing his swimsuit, sandals, and a very damp shirt.

"What's the problem?" I asked, not wanting to know the answer.

"Caleb," said the counselor, "was trying to strangle another camper in the swimming pool—and drown him. So I got him out of the pool and brought him here."

Caleb shot his counselor a defiant glance and then looked down at the floor.

Deeply saddened, I turned to the stone-faced boy in front of me. "Caleb," I said, "we've given you so many chances here at camp this week. This time I'm afraid I'll have to take you home. I'm so sorry."

Caleb briefly raised his eyes. "I don't care!" he literally spat out the words. "I hate everyone here anyway!" Then his thin shoulders sagged under a great wordless weight.

The director was gone for the day and wouldn't be back until late afternoon. I couldn't drive Caleb home until several hours later.

Knowing it was no longer safe to put him back with the other children, I walked him to the craft building, where activities were over for the day. The craft leader was preparing the next day's materials. She agreed to watch over Caleb while I manned the main office until the director's return.

I knew Caleb had no money for buying crafts, so I paid for him to select a ceramic to paint. He chose a dinosaur and fiercely began to paint it fire-engine red.

Later, I loaded Caleb's worn suitcase and little sleeping bag into the trunk of my little car. As we started down the mountain, the boy clutched his red dinosaur and cursed the world. He made frequent references to beatings from his father. He talked about fighting with his brothers. He condemned all the people he planned to kill as soon as he could afford to buy a gun.

Totally out of context, Caleb occasionally reminded me, "Nobody at that camp can make me do anything I don't want to do!"

I didn't know what to say. I was going to be in the car with this child for four hours. When I did speak, I kept my voice low. Most of the time I just prayed. Finally Caleb became quiet and drifted into an exhausted sleep.

New Experiences

The boy awakened an hour and a half later.

"Hungry?" I asked.

Caleb nodded. His eyes grew wide as I pulled into a mountain-side fast-food café.

"I ain't never ate in a restaurant before," he informed me, a tinge of fear in his voice. Cautiously, he followed me inside.

I asked Caleb, "Would you like a sandwich?"

He nodded.

We placed our order and then went to the condiment stand. With ever-widening eyes, he watched me help myself to napkins, packets of ketchup, and straws. "You mean we can just take as many as we want?" he asked.

I smiled and nodded. "Sure. Help yourself."

We sat down at a table to wait for our order and looked out the window in front of us.

Across the road rusty, dented cars slumped among tall weeds outside a rundown motel. Random electrical wires crisscrossed above the dust-covered, wilting summer flowers.

The fast-food chef called that our order was ready. As Caleb devoured his meal, he kept looking at the scene on the other side of the road.

After finishing his food, Caleb was still hungry. I ordered him another sandwich. Halfway through his second sandwich, Caleb swallowed and then became silent. He put his half-eaten sandwich down and looked at me. Then he looked over at the condiment stand. Then he looked out the window at the scene across the road.

In an unexpectedly soft voice he said, "All this is what Paradise must be like."

"Paradise?" I asked, not understanding.

"Yeah, you know—where God lives." Caleb looked across the road again before continuing. "They say there are pretty flowers up there . . . and beautiful big trees . . . and that there's lots of good food to eat."

I listened as the boy continued. "I heard it's quiet up there. No one gets beat up in Paradise." With a note of authority, he added,

"Not with *God* up there, they don't!"

"Caleb," I asked abruptly, "do you want to go to Paradise?"

"Yep," he nodded. "Don't *you?*"

"Sure," I answered, "especially if God—and *you*—are up there."

For the first time that day, Caleb made eye contact with me. A smile slowly stretched across his face. In a bright voice he suddenly observed, "Your napkin looks kinda dirty. Can I get you a new one?"

"Why, thank you," I answered.

With confidence, he walked over to the condiment stand. Then, calling across the room, "Is your straw getting old yet?"

I nodded, and he dove into the straws.

Out of the corner of my eye, I saw him excitedly surveying other containers on the condiment stand. Again, across the room, he almost shouted, "Hey, ever use a toothpick?"

Ignoring other patrons who turned their heads at what had become a very public exchange, I called back, "All the time!"

Quickly Caleb brought me straws, napkins, and toothpicks. With a shy smile of wonder and gratification, he watched me use all these offerings just as quickly and efficiently as I possibly could.

Homeward-bound

During the remainder of our trip together, Caleb didn't make one reference to beatings or people he hated or guns. Instead he talked about loving to watch big birds float in the sky. He said he liked to camp with his oldest brother—and play with the family dogs.

When we arrived at the small house in which he and his mother were temporarily sheltering, Caleb insisted I come in.

"You're probably thirsty and need some water to drink. I'll get it for you."

We stepped inside the front door while I continued to chat with Caleb's weary and disappointed mother.

Caleb darted into one end of the room, which served as a kitchen. He quickly returned with a dirty glass, filled to the brim with lukewarm water.

Without a second thought, I downed it.

Soon I announced I must go, as the drive back to camp would be a long one.

I could tell from the wistful look in Caleb's eyes that he didn't want me to go away. Frankly, I didn't feel so good about leaving him either.

With a sigh I drove away, taking a final mental snapshot over my left shoulder. The little boy and his mother stood by the front picket fence. With one dirty hand Caleb waved. With the other he clutched—close to his heart—a fat, red dinosaur.

I'd left camp earlier that day in the company of a hateful, disturbed, self-centered child. I had completed the trip with a helpful, respectful, and compassionate young man—one who had just caught a glimpse of Paradise.

I believe Caleb had chosen to make some changes that day because he had started to feel loved, no matter what he'd previously done. Having evidence that someone cared gave him hope—not only for eternity but also for the present.

Little Caleb's experience brings us to our final principle for attaining better balance.

Better Balance Principle 4

Growth into Christlike balance will continue as long as I trust God to supply the "glimpses of Paradise" that encourage me to stay committed to Him and His ways (Eph. 3:20).

We can have a well-articulated mission statement.

We can have goals for change in the principal domains of our lives.

We can even have foolproof accountability plans for the changes we want to make.

Yet, all these strategies will be as "sounding brass and tinkling cymbals" unless we let the precious Savior, who's preparing our home in Paradise, first prepare His home in our hearts. He has promised to do so (John 14:23).

What spiritual intimacy we can experience when we talk to Him in prayer, listen to His voice through the Word, and pay attention to His guiding will for the details of our lives!

Paying attention to the details of Christ's words and actions will give us better balance—starting in the heart.

Caleb operated on *feelings* of despair and lack of worthiness. When he focused on the facts—that he was worthy of notice and respect—he was then able to start living above his feelings.

Like Caleb, we can't always afford to depend on feeling. But we *can* always depend on the cross.

We can also depend on the promise Christ made to a newly converted thief hanging from an adjacent cross—the promise that even the most unbalanced among us can still have a future in Paradise.

Believing in the promise of the cross can make all the difference in the world. Just ask Caleb.

HOMEWORK FOR THE HEART

Your Glimpses of Paradise. What glimpses of Paradise—of His love—has God given you? Have you thanked Him recently?

Reminder: To those who are committed to better balance in Him, Christ promises to give motivating and enabling glimpses of Paradise.

---

* E. C. McKenzie, *14,000 Quips and Quotes,* p. 312.

▲

BACK UP ON THE BEAM

ANOTHER SHOT AT STAYING VERTICAL

"In his heart a man plans his course, but the Lord determines his steps."
—*Prov. 16:9, NIV*

"Walk arm in arm with him today. Your eternal escort.
Your faithful bridegroom. He will never let you go."
—*Kathy Troccoli*[1]

THE ABILITY TO CLIMB BACK UP onto the balance beam is only a prayer—
and a choice—away.

The Prayer

When we ask God to be our "spotter" (should we start losing
our balance), He rushes to our side. David quoted God as saying, "I
will set him [representing you and me] on high, because he hath
known my name" (Ps. 91:14). Having God at our side will give us
increasing discernment concerning what to "take off" from our lives
and what to "put on" for better balance than we've had in the past.

After all, God, through Jethro, helped Moses organize a thou-
sand and one details when he was about to go under.

God, through Mordecai, encouraged Queen Esther to focus on
her purpose in the royal house so that she could walk with steady
gait into the throne room to meet either the tip of the royal
scepter—or the business end of the royal sword.

With a lifestyle in which imbalance seemed just a hairbreadth
away, Jesus always relied on God the Father to direct His steps and
order His days. That's why on any given day—no matter what His
"calendar" looked like—He could accommodate an impromptu
night meeting (with Nicodemus, for example), a working lunch

break (with the woman at the well), or a sudden picnic (with more than 5,000).

The Choice

Prayer brings God to the side of our balance beam so that we can complete what *He* wills for our day. And His willing presence at our side gives us a remarkable choice. The choice to reach out by faith and take hold of a nail-scarred hand for the duration of our walk.

Don't get me wrong. You know as well as I that, as frail human beings, we will continue to struggle with imbalance—whether it's caused by our own faults or by the fact that we're living in a sinful world. We may even fall off the beam a few times before getting a better "feel" for staying vertical. (As an anonymous e-mail forward recently reminded me, "Even the sun has a sinking spell once in a while.")

Yet whether we take a sudden tumble or suddenly realize we've quietly slid off, God's hand, tightening around ours, will remind us to keep first things first.

That was certainly Gwen Foster's experience.

As health czar for the city of Philadelphia, Pennsylvania, Gwen was a globe-trotter. While in office she appeared on *The Oprah Winfrey Show,* the *Today Show, Good Morning America,* and *60 Minutes.* She's been featured in the New York *Times, People* magazine, and *USA Today.*

She has also been the cover story of *Women of Spirit* magazine. In an interview that magazine's associate editor asked her, "With such a public and absorbing job, how do you keep first things first?"

Gwen answered, "About 10 years ago my life was out of control. With my previous job I was always on the road, always traveling. I rarely saw my husband. I was out 'saving' the world. I said my family was the most important thing in my life, but my schedule did not demonstrate that."

Gwen began the prayerful and painstaking work of "laying aside." Gwen relates that she decreased her many life roles to seven and then prioritized them, starting with the relationship with her Creator.

I find her following comment particularly reassuring: "I am not always perfect in doing it [keeping all aspects of her life balanced], but I do it more than I don't do it."[2]

Evidently Gwen has discovered the kind of faith King David had when he wrote, "When I said, 'My foot is slipping,' your love, O Lord, supported me. When anxiety was great within me, your consolation brought joy to my soul. . . . The Lord has become my fortress, and my God the rock in whom I take refuge" (Ps. 94:18-22, NIV).

Imitating Christ

We began the first section of this book with an Associated Press story describing how one U.S. Olympic hopeful contributed to her team's low preliminary score. *She lost her balance and fell off the balance beam.*

Near the end of that same article, however, was this sentence, "When finals begin Tuesday, the scores will be wiped clean and the U.S. women will have a chance for a new start, something they could desperately use."[3]

Perhaps *you* could "desperately use" a new start as well. If you feel as if you have been falling off life's balance beam and onto a fast track going nowhere, just remember this. God is more than willing to wipe clean our previous less-than-perfect "scores" and give us a new start. He promises that though we fall, we "shall not be utterly cast down," for He will uphold us "with his hand" (Ps. 37:24).

When Kent was growing up, one of the greatest compliments my little boy could ever pay me was to imitate me. Sometimes he would come out in the kitchen where I was patting out dough for dinner rolls. He'd ask for an apron "just like yours, Mom." Then he'd climb up on a footstool, watch me, and start punching a little clump of dough with his chubby fingers.

Soon he'd be unconsciously spreading flour on his face and in his hair. I noticed but never complained, for he was just learning. He never bristled at my pointers on how to keep more flour on the kneading board and less on the floor. His proud statement was always, "Look! I'm making bread, Mom, just like you." Side by side we'd work. I'd hum a familiar tune. Intermittently he'd glance up, beam broadly through his flour-brushed eyelashes, and say, "I love you, Mom."

In the upper room Jesus demonstrated the importance of "taking off" the unessential—the cumbersome—and "putting on" what was essential for optimum balance.

When we imitate our Savior's example, we, in a sense, are getting up on a little stool beside Him and saying, "I love You, Lord."

The more time we spend in His presence, the more "pointers" He gives us—through His Word, through the unfolding of events in our daily lives, through divine impressions on our hearts during prayer.

Better yet, the more we cling to His hand while moving forward on the balance beam, the more clearly will we understand His heart of love for us.

Now, *that's* a hand worth holding!

HOMEWORK FOR THE HEART

Something to Sing About. Looking back over my self-assessment so far, in what ways do I sense God is leading me forward on life's balance beam? How can I translate my gratitude into effective praise for Him?

Reminder: When we keep hold of the Savior's hand, we can continue to grow into better life balance.

---

[1] Kathy Troccoli, in *God Always Has a Plan B,* p. 22.

[2] Heidi Ford, "Fun, Fit, and Free," *Women of Spirit,* September/October 2002, p. 20.

[3] ESPN Web site, Associated Press story, Sept. 17, 2002.

PART 2

▲

EXERCISING OUR RIGHTS ON GOD'S BALANCE BEAM
(BASED ON JOHN 13:6-11)

In Part 1 we reflected on two significant choices Jesus made in the upper room the night before He was crucified. Within the context of His example, we also assessed our personal state of balance (or imbalance) in five domains of our lives.

We often underscored our discussion, however, by acknowledging that true, lasting balance—as gymnasts on life's balance beam—grows out of an ongoing love relationship with Jesus. The Holy Spirit enables our better balance as we come to know and understand our Savior at a deeper level.

What's so exciting about being one of God's balance beam gymnasts is that He gives us special rights to exercise. Exercising these privileges brings even more focused balance to our lives.

At least two years prior to the upper room experience Christ gave His disciples certain authority. Matthew 10:1 records He gave them "power" before sending them out on their first missionary endeavors. Again, just before He returned to heaven, Christ empowered His disciples (which includes us, this time) with the authorization and rights for fulfilling His personal commission to each of us.

When we exercise these rights on life's balance beam, our feet on that "straight and narrow" grow steadier with each successive step.

In Part 2 we will look at some of these rights so significant to God's end-time gymnasts.

Reminder: God's balance beam gymnasts have God-given rights to exercise.

▲

CHAPTER 15

LARRY BOY AND BETTINA

OUR RIGHT TO RESIST

"Resist the devil, and he will flee from you."
—James 4:7

"It takes more courage to resist by faith than to keep on sinning."
—Unknown

IN THE UPPER ROOM THAT EVENING Christ prepared Himself to serve His disciples. Specifically, to wash their dirty feet. He had taken off garments that would have gotten in the way of His kneeling on the floor. He had girded Himself with a towel. As usual, He was perfectly balanced in His Father and ready for anything.

Petty arguments and small talk died on the lips of His disciples, for the Master lifted a servant's pitcher and poured water into a basin. He knelt before the first disciple and swished clean water over the dust-caked ankles and toes.

We don't know who that first disciple was, yet we can imagine that all watched in awkward silence as the Master quietly modeled something so foreign to their human natures—humility.

Scripture records the response of just one disciple, Simon Peter. When Christ knelt before him, Peter resisted the Master's kind offer. "Lord, are you going to wash my feet? . . . No, . . . you shall never wash my feet" (John 13:6-8, NIV).

God has always given His children the right to resist certain things: temptations, negative attitudes, and besetting sins.

Yet Peter misused this right. He used it to reject something Christ wanted to do *for* him!

How often I have resisted the Holy Spirit in my life instead of resisting what God counsels me to resist. A calf taught me the folly—and accompanying danger—of resisting the wrong things.

Larry Boy

A while back one of our cows gave birth to a baby bull. We named him Larry Boy. He had such big brown eyes. I started talking to him more than to the other calves and giving him a bit of extra grain.

When I mentioned Larry Boy's cute ways to my neighbor, who has raised cattle for years, she gave me this warning: "Carolyn, be careful that you don't get too friendly with any one calf. When it gets bigger, it gets pushier. That could lead to real problems down the road."

Eh, she might be right, I thought, *but Larry Boy is so cute and so little!* I quietly resisted her advice.

Several months later, after the calves were weaned, we decided to use their lawn-mowing services in a pasture where the tall, dry grass was becoming a fire hazard. Jim went to the other end of the pasture to close a gate while I opened the entrance gate for the calves. They each weighed more than 500 pounds now, Larry being by far the heaviest. Without incident they followed me through the gate into the new pasture and began grazing.

I was heading toward the gate nearest the house when I suddenly heard a thick snort behind me. Looking over my shoulder, I saw Larry Boy coming after me at a fast walk. He tossed his head over his shoulder, as he did when he heard the grain bucket. I was amazed at how large he appeared when no fence separated us. I grew a bit uneasy.

He continued closing the gap between us. When I stopped, he stopped. When I walked, he walked. Concerned that he might gain momentum and bump into me, I wheeled around, gestured broadly, and barked an authoritative "No!"

Larry Boy stopped in his tracks and inhaled deeply before exhaling another impatient snort. To my consternation, he started pawing the ground with one of his front hooves.

He wanted all of my attention and was ready to play.

My husband, who had noticed Larry's aggressive behavior, now came hurrying into the pasture. There he distracted Larry so I could get to the gate.

Two days later, when I started out on my morning walk, I heard a familiar and excited "Moo." Larry Boy stood with the other grazing calves at the far side of their new pasture.

I hollered, "Good morning!" and continued my brisk pace.

The next thing I felt was the ground vibrating beneath my feet as Larry Boy thundered toward me across the turf. I turned to see nearly 600 pounds of raw beef coming at me full-bore. The barbed-wire fence between us suddenly seemed very fragile.

Larry skidded to a quick halt just before arriving at the fence. I quickened my pace. Larry trotted alongside me just on the other side of the barbed wire. Maneuvering around two skinny trees in his path, he galloped ahead, then turned to face me as I proceeded down this deserted stretch of road. He playfully tossed his massive head.

Warning Recalled

Too late I recalled the warning of my neighbor—the warning I had not only resisted but rejected. "Be careful that you don't get too friendly with any one calf," she had said. "For when it gets bigger, it gets pushier. That could lead to real problems down the road."

Well, guess what? Here I was, literally down the road, and a big problem was snorting and pawing the ground just yards from me.

With a hind-leg power kick, Larry Boy lunged, arching his back like a rodeo bull. Then he twisted his body in the air, whirled, landed, and, in great zigzags, raced toward the other calves like a joyful puppy. I took off down the road at a racewalker's pace.

Nostrils flaring, Larry Boy rounded the far corner of the pasture and started back toward me with the other calves now in tow. Just then I reached the point in the road where our pasture ends and the neighbor's pasture begins. Very quickly I put a great distance between Larry Boy and me.[1]

On my alternate route home, I had time to reflect on a lesson the oversized calf had just demonstrated for me. What Larry Boy taught me is that when I misuse my right to resist, by resisting my heavenly Neighbor, I have a big problem. If I hold on to even one little cherished sin, that sin starts wanting to hold on to me. Like Larry, it will grow bigger and stronger and become more demanding of my time, energy, and attention. Eventually, if I don't resist it, that small indulgence will want—and eventually take—all of me.

In stark contrast to the decision I'd made (to resist my neighbor's advice) stands Bettina. She exercised her God-given right to resist, but in a positive way. And what a difference that has made in many lives!

Bettina

My husband and I met Bettina during a short-term mission trip to Micronesia. I'll never forget the day she shared her testimony with us. Jim and I had finished our speaking commitments and were guests on a one-day snorkeling outing midst the beautiful islands of Palau. Bettina was one of our hostesses aboard the boat.

At a snorkeling stop, where jade-green islands dotted the seascape under a clear blue sky, she and I stood in waist-deep water. Schools of exotic and curious fish swarmed about our feet and legs, snatching grains of rice we dropped into the warm waters.

When I asked Bettina, "Have you always been a Christian?" she began sharing.

Though raised a Christian, Bettina had somehow drifted away from her upbringing. In fact, for a number of years she had worked her way up in a major international airline. Eventually her job necessitated a move from Palan to Saipan. Her job-related perks included free airline tickets, so she also traveled extensively.

"I stopped resisting the attractions of the world," she said. "I was addicted to a number of substances, betel nut being the strongest one. I also loved putting on heavy makeup in order to look glamorous."

She continued, "I thought my life had the best of everything, but every once in a while I noticed a deep emptiness—even with a lot of friends partying around me."

A member of Bettina's family back in Palau fell ill and died. On the red-eye flight back to Saipan the night following the funeral, Bettina reflected on her late relative. *I wonder if he was ready to die.*

Quickly another thought followed. *Would I be ready to die?*

Her honest answer was a resounding no. Suddenly that sensation of strange emptiness engulfed her. Once again an icy loneliness clutched her stomach as she thought about her destination: Saipan, where she would be caught up in the same old round of fleetingly pleasurable, but meaningless, activities. With all her vices, Bettina feared asking to be God's child again would be hypocritical. Yet she saw that her failure to resist dabbling in sin had led to her complete slavery to sin.

Suddenly she felt exhausted and longed to change her lifestyle. *But how can I ask God to take me back when my list of sins is so long?* she wondered.

A Bible verse she'd memorized as a child flashed into her mind: *"If we confess our sins, he is faithful and just to forgive us our sins, and to cleanse us from all unrighteousness."*

In the subdued interior light of that midnight flight, Bettina opened her expensive brand-name black leather purse and surveyed its contents. Most of the items represented some of her enslavements: apparatus for making betel-nut chews, a pack of cigarettes, and several cases of garish makeup.

She thought, *It's my choice to keep these or reject them.*

Midnight Conversion

From her purse, Bettina removed her passport and wallet. These she slipped into her pocket., then snapped her purse shut.

Apologetically climbing over a dozing seatmate, Bettina made her way down the darkened aisle past sleeping passengers. She didn't stop until she reached the flight attendants' galley. There, through a little swinging door to a concealed trash receptacle, Bettina dumped her old life—purse and all.

By the time Bettina returned to her row, tears flowed down her cheeks. Stifling sobs, she climbed over her seatmate. Not caring what he might think, she slid onto her knees. In her cramped confessional, Bettina rejected her past life of sin, accepted Heaven's forgiveness, and asked God to give her the power to resist her former enslavements.

"Resist the devil," wrote James, "and he will flee from you" (James 4:7). Peter, who had resisted Christ in the upper room later reminded five different regions (1 Peter 1:1) that resisting the enemy is a right that we *must* exercise (1 Peter 5:9).

"I don't remember how long I knelt there in the plane," Bettina told me, "but I felt that familiar longtime emptiness just *fill up* with God!"

A New Walk

During the remainder of our snorkeling day together, Bettina told me more about God's subsequent leading in her life. How He had provided for her needs when she quit her lucrative job over day-of-worship issues.

She shared how, in the next four months, God blessed her first-love witnessing. Bettina felt impressed to start holding Bible studies. In a matter of months, as a direct result of her studies, 30 new members joined the little church she attended.

Bettina told us how God had opened the way for her to go to the Philippines to pursue certified training in Bible work.

"My old friends think I'm crazy to walk away from all that was mine. They thought I was crazy to start spending so much time in God's Word. But I love it! I knew I needed its power to help me reject what separated me from Him. I'm so happy He gives me power to resist the pleasures of the world!"

It's Our Right

How exactly do we go about resisting? Again, Christ—through His earthly example—showed us how.

"By what means did He overcome in the conflict with Satan? By the word of God. Only by the word could He resist temptation. 'It is written,' He said. And unto us are given 'exceeding great and precious promises: that by these ye might be partakers of the divine nature, having escaped the corruption that is in the world through lust' (2 Peter 1:4). Every promise in God's word is ours. . . . When assailed by temptation, look not to circumstances or to the weakness of self, but to the power of the word. All its strength is yours. 'Thy word,' says the psalmist, 'have I hid in mine heart, that I might not sin against thee' (Ps. 119:11)."[2]

Spending time in God's Word will equip us to know *how* to exercise our right to resist. God's Spirit, through His Word, will also give us the necessary discernment to know what to resist so that we make the Bettina, rather than the Larry Boy, choices. (We'll discuss discernment in more depth in a subsequent chapter.)

HOMEWORK FOR THE HEART

What's That in *Your* Purse? Bettina not only rid herself of what she'd previously valued above God, but she threw out the whole purse!

Spiritually speaking, what do you have in your purse that you need to resist or even dump out? You might read Psalm 51 and talk to God about how it relates to certain details in your life.

Reminder: God's goodness enables us to resist whatever would get between Him and us.

---

[1] By the way, I don't know where Larry is anymore. About a week after my troubling encounters with the young bull, a neighbor asked to purchase him for another herd. The last time we saw the demanding, never-satisfied Larry, he was happily trotting down the road behind the neighbor's ATV, trying to get close enough to stick his nose into the grain bucket.

[2] Ellen G. White, *The Desire of Ages,* p. 123.

CHAPTER 16

▲

DEALING WITH FOUL ODORS

OUR RIGHT TO BREATHE FREE

*"If we confess our sins, he is faithful and just to forgive us our sins,
and to cleanse us from all unrighteousness."*
—1 John 1:9

"Guilt stinks!"
—Unknown

THE PREVIOUS CHAPTER REMINDED US THAT, through His Son's death on the cross, God gives each of us the right to resist anything that would get in the way of a deeper relationship with Him.

Yet, because we were born with sinful tendencies, we have made multiple choices not to exercise this right. In fact, we, like Peter, have—time and again—resisted the wooing of the Holy Spirit instead of resisting the promptings of the enemy.

The next thing we know the enemy turns on us, using our guilty consciences to condemn us for making the foolish, selfish choices that have damaged both ourselves and others.

In fact, right now you may be asking yourself questions such as these:

How can God truly love and accept me when my stupid past choices still affect my children so deeply?

How can God be with me during this illness when I know it's possibly the direct result of an unhealthful lifestyle?

Can God possibly love—much less save—me when I knowingly walked away from Him and His help in order to gratify my own desires?

Some of us have experienced guilt that lingers—sometimes for years—like a foul odor.

Choices That Led to the Bad Smell

The president of a rich Western country appointed a young diplomat, whom I'll call Ambassador New, to serve in the same landlocked African country where we were missionaries. (The following incident filtered down through the local grapevine.)

Soon after taking over his new appointment, Ambassador New decided he needed a customized Lincoln Continental limousine instead of the used Mercedes-Benz the previous ambassador maintained. So he ordered one from the United States.

As soon as Ambassador New received word that his limousine had arrived at the Kenyan port of Mombasa, he dispatched his newly hired indigenous chauffeur to go pick it up. He also granted permission for the chauffeur's brother to go along and help drive.

Three days later the two brothers were heading home in the ambassador's shiny black limo. Since they planned to drive night and day in order to meet Ambassador New's stringent time constraints, they stopped to purchase food at Nairobi's huge outdoor market.

Walking between hundreds of produce vendors in search of "fast-food" stands, the brothers passed a farmer's wife selling chickens.

"Brother!" exclaimed the chauffeur to his sibling, "look how inexpensive chickens are here compared to the ones back home. My wife would love a few for eggs and stew."

"So would mine!" the brother concurred. "But," he paused a second, "where would we put them for transport?"

"Do you and I take up *all* the room in that new car we're driving?" asked the chauffeur, an edge of sarcasm in his voice. "Surely we have room for a few chickens."

"Of course we do!" his brother agreed enthusiastically. "Since we ride in the driver's compartment, we can put the chickens back where the ambassador and his guests will travel and keep the partition closed."

"I'll take three fat chickens," the chauffeur informed the vendor before continuing conversation with his brother. "We'll just throw a little cracked corn on the floor—and put down a pan of water. The chickens will be fine."

His brother nodded before turning to the vendor. "I'll take three chickens as well." Then he turned to his brother and said, "They'll have plenty of room to move around on the floor, the seat, and in the back window. And the air-conditioning will keep them from dying of the heat."

The two men transported their upside-down chickens, legs tied together, to the ambassador's new car. There they released them into the passenger compartment. After situating a pan of water on the floor's plush carpet, they scattered several handfuls of newly purchased corn about the floor and across the back seats. Then they slammed the door and continued their drive.

The next day, while traversing a neighboring country, they came upon another large market. The chauffeur screeched to a halt. He said to his brother, "Go quickly and see what they're asking for chickens here."

Breathlessly his brother returned. "They're cheaper here than in Kenya!"

The chauffeur dug into his pocket and gave his brother a handful of bills. "Get me three more chickens." While awaiting his brother, the chauffeur threw more corn on the rear compartment carpet, now soggy from water that had splashed out of the pan—not to mention a thin layer of fresh chicken droppings.

Soon the chauffeur's brother returned with an upside-down fluttering "bouquet" of chickens in each hand. "I got *my* wife more chickens, as well," he announced.

The two men carefully released six cackling hens into the rear compartment. Now, back in the diplomatic compartment, one dozen chickens simultaneously bounced, floundered, and squawked every time the long limo jounced over one of the numerous potholes riddling the unpaved road.

Twenty hours later, near midnight, an embassy night watchman swung wide the front gate to Ambassador New's diplomatic compound. The chauffeur carefully drove in. He and his brother quickly left the limo keys with the night watchman, collected their chickens, and went home.

Early next morning Ambassador New arrived at the embassy in a flurry of excitement. "Open the back door to my limousine," he ordered a saluting aide. "I want to check it out." The diplomat stooped and slid inside the passenger's compartment.

Suddenly—and backwards—Ambassador New shot out of the limousine, holding his nose.

"Whew!" he roared. "What's *that* in my new car?"

Word trickled down through the jungle grapevine that even after multiple cleanings, embassy employees could not rid the limo interior of its distinctive feathery fragrance.

Though the chickens were long gone, no one could eliminate the olfactory evidence of their earlier presence.

When Chickens Come Home to Roost

Word soon spread throughout the countryside about Ambassador New being stuck with a stinking limousine—the very one he had been so hasty to order for himself. His predicament—for a time, anyway—was the funniest joke around.

However, living with the aromatic aftermath of his arrogant choice was no laughing matter to the ambassador.

And so it is often with us. The "chickens" in our past—those spur-of-the-moment, sinful choices—are history. Yet, the "aroma"—the lingering reminders—of their earlier presence in our lives remains in the form of guilt feelings. These feelings, along with our accusing memories, cling to us like a bad odor. Unresolved guilt throws us off balance both spiritually and emotionally because it weighs us down. It distracts us from fully living in the present. Because feelings of guilt are attached to past actions that we cannot change, we fear we must bear them for life.

Yet we don't have to.

We don't have to bear our guilt any more than Ambassador New had to keep inhaling chicken-waste-scented air. He found a way to escape the noxious fumes of the past. His new nickname said it all. People in the countryside began referring to the diplomat as "The Ambassador Who Always Travels With His Windows Rolled Down."

Sometimes he even opened the limousine's sunroof and stood up. Head and shoulders protruding in the sunshine, he'd waved to onlookers as his country's mounted flags proudly waved from the hood.

Even though the ambassador was stuck with nasal reminders from an irrevocable past choice, he could still pump his lungs full of fresh air and get on with his life. Inevitably someone in the roadside crowd gathered for a parade or an official diplomatic cavalcade would remark, "Look at him smile! He's risen above the stench."

Spiritually speaking, how *do* we rise above the stench of past guilt and regret?

Perhaps this experience of a former student will illustrate how we can do this.

Expensive Choice

One day Michael (as I will call him) received our school's permission to take a music department sousaphone home. He needed to practice for an upcoming band concert. Michael promised to guard the instrument with his life.

After school that day Michael hauled the sousaphone to the bench of the nearest public bus stop just outside the front door of a convenience store.

Buses were running late that day. Soon the fidgeting Michael tired of visiting with a classmate who was also awaiting a bus. Through the open doors of the store Michael could hear the voices of two other classmates playing a video game.

"Watch my instrument a minute, will ya?" Michael said to his classmate. "I want to go inside and play a game or two."

"Sure," responded his friend. "But if my bus comes first, I'm outta here."

"No problem," said Michael. "I'll be watching." Michael joined his friends inside and played only two video games before sticking his head out the door to see if his bus was coming yet. He saw no bus, and no friend, and, to his horror, no sousaphone. After his friend's departure, a passing opportunist had left with the school's expensive sousaphone.

When Michael dragged into my classroom the following morning, his posture and pale complexion suggested he wasn't feeling well.

"Are you catching a cold or the flu?" I asked him.

"I feel sort of sick" was all he would say.

The next day, when his condition didn't appear to have improved, I asked Michael to stay after class for a moment. I quietly asked him to tell me what was bothering him. He told me about the stolen sousaphone.

"I was so stupid to leave the instrument on the bench!" he moaned. "The school will want us to pay, but my mother doesn't have the money. She's already working two jobs and really stressed. My chest feels tight all the time. I feel so guilty I can't eat or sleep!"

"I'm really sorry," I said. "But you've got to deal with this. You can't go through life with a tight chest and not eating or sleeping. So what do you think you need to do to change how you feel?"

He groaned. "Nothing can ever change how bad I feel. But I guess I do need to talk to the principal."

"That would certainly be the place to start," I encouraged him.

"But she'll *kill* me!" he wailed.

"No, she won't," I promised.

"Would you go to the principal's office with me—and just be there with me so she won't kill me when I tell her?"

A few minutes later the principal motioned for us to take seats in front of her desk.

"Michael has something to tell you," I said as a non-too-subtle hint for him to start talking.

Michael swallowed hard and then told the principal what had happened.

The more he talked, the more upset she became. In fact, I'd never seen her so agitated. When Michael paused momentarily, she verbally lit into him with an accusatory lecture about everything he'd done wrong. Then she predicted what negative consequences would befall him once the school board got hold of the news.

Finally she excused herself to "go cool down."

Her intense emotional response shocked me. Even *I* was near tears.

Michael sat in dead silence. Then I heard him release a sigh not unlike air escaping from a punctured tire.

I said a silent prayer before glancing sideways at him.

Instead of being slumped over in his chair, as he'd been in my classroom a few minutes earlier, Michael had slid way down—almost on his back. His head rested comfortably against the chair. His eyes were closed and a peaceful half smile swathed his face.

"Michael," I tentatively asked, "are you all right?"

"Ah," he said lazily, letting another deep sign escape his lips. "That felt *sooo good!*"

"What felt good?" I asked.

"What just happened in here," he answered. "No matter what happens next, that terrible secret is off my chest. I feel as though—as though I can *breathe* again!"

Breathing Free

Michael could not change what he had done, but he *could* unload his sense of heavy guilt by confessing his wrong.

One of the hardest lessons we learn in life is that we cannot change the past. Neither can God change it because He has given us the freedom of choice.

Yet Calvary can *free* us from living with lingering guilt from the past.

Do you remember how Ambassador New avoided breathing the foul odors while in his limousine? He simply rolled down the windows in preparation for fresh air to blow through.

In a sense, we roll down the windows of our souls when we confess to God our failure at resisting sin.

In response to our confession, God's Spirit—like a sweet, cleansing breeze—blows through the windows of our memories and souls, carrying away the stench (John 3:8).

God calls this process forgiveness. As His goodness enables our repentance (Rom. 2:4), His Son enables our forgiveness. "The God of our fathers raised up Jesus. . . . Him hath God exalted with his right hand to be a Prince and a Saviour, for to give repentance to Israel, and forgiveness of sins" (Acts 5:30, 31).

How grateful I am to know that as long as I keep the soul's windows open—confessing sin and receiving forgiveness for it—the foul odors of regret, sorrow, and guilt can no longer overwhelm me (1 John 1:9).

As with Michael, we will wear the smile of relief, which comes from having a clear conscience.

We will be like Ambassador New—standing vertical, head and shoulders through the sunroof and face to the wind—riding through life sustained by cleansing infusions of forgiveness.

When heavenly onlookers watch us go by, I'm sure they will nod joyfully and say, "Look at her smile! Look at him! They've risen above the stench!"

You can get rid of that stifling guilt! Exercise your right to breathe free!

HOMEWORK FOR THE HEART

Getting Rid of Guilt. What have you been carrying around in your official Guilt Continental? Why not deal with it, as Michael did in the principal's office? Realize that you *can't* change the past, but that you *can* shift its aftermath from your shoulders into the hands of God.

Reminder: Through our confession and God's forgiveness, we can unload guilt from past poor choices and get on with our lives.

▲

CHAPTER 17

LESSONS FROM THE SHUNAMMITE

OUR RIGHT TO PERSIST, PART 1

*"We are made partakers of Christ, if we hold
the beginning of our confidence stedfast unto the end."*
—The apostle Paul*

"Great tasks are never completed if you give up at the last minute."
—Something I've learned the hard way

AMONG THE ESSENTIAL QUALITIES FOR SUCCESS on the balance beam is persistence. If a gymnast doesn't doggedly train, practice, and endlessly repeat her routines, she risks future imbalance and even a fall off the beam.

A lack of persistence in any significant area of life can cause failure. I know. I'm dealing with that reality right now in my very own kitchen!

You see, the windup timer sitting on my stove is driving me crazy! Oh, it ticks away faithfully enough, whether I set it for four minutes or 54 minutes. The problem is that it faithfully ticks *until* the very last minute. Then it stops—right before the dinger goes off.

If I'm in another room or talking on the phone, I don't hear the ticking stop. My husband is getting tired of charcoal-edged garlic bread that remained under the broiler a few minutes too long—because the timer didn't *persist* in seeing its job through to the end.

Sometimes I too have a problem with giving up too soon. Especially when I get tired or overwhelmed or a situation suddenly seems hopeless. However, at times like these an unnamed woman in the Old Testament reminds me of yet another right that God has given us. The right to *persist* in trusting the only One who can keep us vertical on the balance beam—come what may.

Encouraging Model of Persistence

I first met this young woman in 2 King 4. The Scripture writer refers to her only as the Shunammite woman. He notes the woman was kind and hospitable. For example, when she observed the prophet Elisha often passing through her village of Shunem with no place to stay, she consulted her husband about their providing for the man of God.

With the blessing of her husband, the Shunammite prepared an upstairs guest quarters that had its own outside entrance (verses 9, 10).

In return for her kindness, Elisha asked the Shunammite what she might desire in return for her kindness. She answered simply, "I dwell among my own people—I have no need of anything." Her response to the prophet shows that her outwardly kind gesture was not in expectation of a special favor in return from anyone—even from God. She served others simply to honor God (verse 9).

When Gehazi, Elisha's servant, pointed out that the woman was childless and that her husband was elderly, Elisha asked God to bless the woman by giving her a child (verses 16-18). God answered the prophet's prayer.

Several years later the Shunammite's growing son suffered a heat stroke one day out in the field where he was helping his father. Though the young mother administered first aid, her son still died within a few hours. Here's where this sad story gets exciting—and amazing!

Senseless Act of Trust

The Shunammite could have said, "Oh, well, so much for the prophet's bed-and-breakfast arrangement. I'm hanging up my faith and turning that little upstairs chamber into a sewing nook." Instead, as a daughter of God, she exercised her right to persist in trusting Him.

She saddled up behind a servant and thundered off to the prophet's permanent lodging. Elisha had no idea why his normally circumspect hostess was so wild-eyed. In amazement he watched the Shunammite throw herself on the ground before him and—to his servant's chagrin—grab the prophet's ankles.

As soon as the woman blurted out her anguish, Elisha dispatched Gehazi, his servant, to the guest quarters in Shunem. "Lay my staff on the boy's face," he commanded.

At this point the woman could have parted company with the prophet and returned home to see what would happen. Instead she declared to Elisha, "As surely as the Lord lives and as you live, I will not leave you" (verse 30, NIV).

Quickly Elisha accompanied the woman back to Shunem. There God rewarded her persistent faith through Elisha when the prophet—not his rod—raised the little boy back to life.

The Rest of the Story

But wait! That isn't the end of the story! The Shunammite shows up four chapters later in the first few verses of 2 Kings 8. In this part of the narrative a number of factors have changed in her life. She is much older and most certainly widowed.

One characteristic, however, has not changed. She is still exercising her God-given right to persist in trusting His faithfulness.

Israel had fallen on hard times during a seven-year drought. Foreseeing the famine, Elisha had counseled the woman to move to the land of the Philistines until the drought ended (verse 1). Upon returning to Israel, the woman and her son discovered that a non-family member had confiscated both her house and all her land. The helpless widow decided to appeal her case to the king.

God's timing is precise. At the exact moment the Shunammite entered the hearing chamber of the king, Gehazi, Elisha's former servant, just "happened" to be there at the king's request. For the king, having heard of the late prophet's miracles, had requested a firsthand account.

Gehazi was in the middle of the story of how the prophet had restored the Shunammite's son to life. At that very instant the man looked up and cried out as if he'd seen a ghost.

"My lord, O king, this is the woman, and this is her son, whom Elisha restored to life" (verse 5, KJV).

Astounded, the king asked the Shunammite woman to validate Gehazi's account. She did—and then added the latest chapter about the illegal squatters being on her property. The king, deeply moved by her thrilling account of God's faithfulness in her life, quickly assigned a special court officer to the woman's civil case. His orders were as follows: "Restore all that was hers and all the produce of the field from the day that she left the land even until now" (verse 6, NASB).

Throughout Scripture God validates individuals who exercise their right to persist in trusting Him with those setbacks in life that throw one off balance. When we persist in trust, we will also persist in prayer (James 5:16), in obedience (John 14:23), and in service to others (1 Peter 2:12).

Persistent trust deepens our relationship with Him. Paul puts it this way: "We have come to share in Christ if we *hold firmly till the end* the confidence we had at first" (Heb. 3:14, NIV).

When we're staying vertical on the balance beam, we'll discover something else about our Savior—*He's* persistent too.

HOMEWORK FOR THE HEART

Being Persistent. Positive persistence is catching! You might be interested to know that the Shunammite's exact words to Elisha at the height of her anguish were the *exact* words Elisha kept repeating to Elijah (2 Kings 2:2, 4, 6)—just before Elijah's translation to heaven.

Another persistent character in this story was Elisha himself, who persisted with God on the Shunammite's behalf (see 2 Kings 4:32-36). Today we might refer to this type of persistence as intercessory prayer.

For what or whom would you like to "persist with God" right now?

---

* Heb. 3:14.

▲

CHAPTER 18

MARY AND ME

OUR RIGHT TO PERSIST, PART 2

"Failure is the path of least persistence."★

As I MENTIONED EARLIER, I sometimes need to shake up my kitchen timer when it stops being persistent. Likewise, God sometimes needs to shake up persistence-challenged people. That's what He did to Peter in the upper room the night before the Crucifixion. And He did it with persistence.

When the bickering disciples repaired to the upper room in preparation for their meal, no servant met them with a water basin or a towel. But Jesus did.

He continued washing His disciples' feet until He, at last, knelt before Peter. Riddled with guilt that his and Christ's places weren't reversed, Peter quickly asked, "Lord, are you going to wash my feet?" (John 13:6, NIV). Then he added, "You shall never wash my feet" (verse 8, NIV).

Though he was recoiling at Christ's pure hands touching his filthy feet, Peter, in a sense, was also refusing to let Christ wash his heart.

Jesus explained that Peter might not understand what He was doing until later. "Unless I wash you, you have no part with me" (John 13:8, NIV).

Christ's authoritative statement jolted Peter into hastily declaring, "Then, Lord, . . . not just my feet but my hands and my head as well!" (verse 9, NIV).

MARY AND ME ▸ 119

Patiently, persistently, Christ talked to Peter, reminding him that though he had already "had a bath," his feet still retained new dust from the day's journey.

At last, the headstrong disciple submitted to Christ's persistence.

As with Peter, we don't always appreciate or understand heaven's persistence on our behalf. Yet the end results may surprise us, as they did me when I lived above an annoyingly persistent neighbor

Pesky Persistence

Stride-stride-stride. I operated the hand-me-down exercise machine in my new third-story apartment.

Bang-bang-bang!

Something like a broomstick handle thumped the ceiling of the apartment underneath mine. The next thing I knew, someone was thumping on my front door.

"You—too noisy!" exclaimed a large woman with a thick accent. She subsequently identified herself as Mary, the neighbor living in the apartment beneath mine.

"Rau-rau-rau!" she intoned, imitating the disrupting noise she claimed I'd been making. At the same time she gestured alternately and rhythmically with her hands that she held in the shape of claws.

I demonstrated for her the smooth, innocent action of my exerciser, but she just shook her head. "I no like big loud up here! Not good!"

While she scolded me, I made a mental note to store my convenient in-house exerciser and take up bicycle riding—outside. Br-r-r!

I profusely apologized to her. Then endeavoring to show that I meant no harm, I handed her my telephone number.

Big mistake!

A week later when I tried to practice my saxophone quietly, Mary phoned.

"Now you make big car-horn traffic noise?" she asked. "Wah-wah-wah!"

I thanked her for letting me know the sound carried through the floor. Then I stuffed hand towels into the bell of the instrument as a mute.

A week later when I took my banjo out of its case for the first time in years, the phone rang again.

Mary was on the other end of the line—of course. "Tat-a-tat-a-tat!" she complained. *"New noisy now!"*

I clipped clothespins onto the banjo bridge to deaden the percussive vibrations from the instrument's sounding board. From then on I practiced music sitting on a straight-backed chair in the bathroom. A thick throw rug on the floor and the whirring bathroom fan turned on high finally camouflaged any stray notes.

Mary stopped complaining—about music, that is. One evening my four quiet, well-mannered French students came over to prepare *la cuisine française* in my kitchen. We'd barely begun our meal preparation when the telephone rang.

"You have big party!" accused Mary at the other end of the line. "How many people you got dancing on kitchen floor?"

I assured her we were doing only minimal walking from the kitchen to the table. I could tell by her grunt, however, that she didn't believe me.

One evening, when I'd been quietly sitting at my table paying bills for the past two hours, the new neighbors across the hall bumped or dropped something. The resulting boom vibrated the floor beneath my feet. Next they cranked up their sound system.

I started a mental countdown. *7 . . . 6 . . . 5 . . . 4 . . .*

"You dropping big furniture now?" called Mary through my door, simultaneously pounding on it.

Shaking my head, I slowly got up from the table. Framed by the doorway, Mary watched me point to the piles of paper. "Mary," I said after defending myself, "this time that noise you heard came from that apartment *over there.*"

She glared at me.

Then, with perfect timing, the explosive vibration from the apartment across the hall repeated itself, shaking the floor beneath our feet.

A look of surprise and understanding came over Mary's face.

I nodded toward the opposite doorway. Mary zoomed across the hall and pounded on that door. "You dropping *furniture* in there?" she roared.

With a little smile of vindication, I quietly closed my door.

The day I moved away from that apartment complex, I went downstairs to say goodbye to Mary. I wouldn't have—had she not been so persistent for four years. Without her incessant phone calls and visits, I would never have known about her health problems—or her loneliness—or her love for Jesus. I would never have taken her flowers—and she would never have shared homemade cookies with me.

Had Mary not been so persistent, I wouldn't have learned to pray for her—or she for me. If it hadn't been for her frequent "shaking" me up, I wouldn't have told her I wanted to be her neighbor in heaven. And she wouldn't have said "I love you" and cried when I said goodbye.

Through Mary's persistence God persistently softened my heart. Though far from perfect, I'd become a much more sensitive neighbor than I'd been four years earlier when first moving into that apartment complex.

As with my neighbor Mary, God's persistence may feel at times like harassment. Yet, on "moving day," we will finally understand that, all along, His dogged persistence was just another manifestation of grace.

His Ways

God asks us to be persistent because He is. He persisted in walking toward the cross in our place. Still He persists in forgiving our countless sins. He persists in offering us second chances (Ps. 103:10-12). He persists in quietly opening before us His unfolding plans for our lives, though we, like Peter, may not always be quick to catch on. Always, He persists in steadying our uncertain steps during times of imbalance.

Remember my malfunctioning kitchen timer? Well, it eventually broke down, so I replaced it with a new one—just like Jesus began doing with the heart of Peter when it started breaking in front of the kneeling Savior. By Sunday morning Peter had a brand-new heart—one that would persistently "tick" until its work for the Master was done.

Jesus wants to do the same for you.

HOMEWORK FOR THE HEART
Persistently Persistent. You've heard the expression "Using muscles strengthens them." God actually encourages us to practice persistence. Read the parable of the persistent widow in Luke 18:1-5.

Now, about what aspect in your life do you want to be more

persistent? _____

_____ .

Ask the persistent God for strength to persist.
Reminder: Our God persists in refining us for our present good, for the advancement of His kingdom on earth, and for our eternal happiness.

_____

★ E. C. McKenzie, *14,000 Quips and Quotes,* p. 391.

▲

CHAPTER 19

OF FISHERMEN AND PHOTOGRAPHERS

OUR RIGHT TO DISCERN

"O ye hypocrites, ye can discern the face of the sky;
but can ye not discern the signs of the times?"
—Matt. 16:3

"Men of good judgment seldom rely wholly on their own."
—Anonymous★

ONE OF OUR MOST USEFUL—AND COMPLEX—PRIVILEGES is the right to discern (tell the difference between).

We exercise this right in a number of ways.

- We discern where we actually are versus where we think we are.
- We discern fact from fiction.
- We discern reality from perception.
- We discern what is important from that which isn't.
- We discern between God's ways and ours.

Not exercising one's right to discern reaps results that run the gamut from mild embarrassment to grim, life-impacting outcomes. I present the following exhibits, both contemporary and biblical.

Exhibit A: The Floundering Fisherman
(Discerning Where We Are)

The local Search and Rescue Department in the mountains where I once lived received a missing person's alert. They quickly organized a team to search for a missing fisherman.

Rescuers soon found the footprints of the missing fisherman. They led upstream from a favorite fishing hole of his. About three miles into rough wilderness, they came upon the missing fisherman. He was methodically tossing leaves into the stream.

"What are you doing?" inquired the rescue leader.

The man replied, "I'm keeping tabs on which direction is north."

"With your compass?"

"No," answered the man. "I don't need one. I use the floating leaf method for finding my directions."

"What do you mean?" asked the leader.

"Well," answered the man, "I once heard that when you throw leaves into a stream, they always go south. I'm lost and I need to go north. So if I can find where south is, I can find my car from here."

After much arguing, search team members convinced the fisherman to walk back down the trail with them. They took him directly to his parked car.

Two weeks later Search and Rescue received another missing person's bulletin—the same fisherman was missing again and in the same area. The team went directly to his favorite fishing hole. Sure enough, he was once again tossing leaves into the stream.

This time he agreed to purchase a compass and learn how to use it before going on a weekend solo fishing trip again. He made this discerning remark: "I suppose *knowing* where I am could help me stay out of trouble."

How true!

Exhibit B: Bill Gates, Mickey Mouse, and Me (Discerning Fact From Fiction)

All right, go ahead and admit it. If you have e-mail service, you've probably fallen prey to at least one hoax, as I did.

An acquaintance, whom I knew and trusted, e-mailed a forward to me. It stated, on the authority of "reliable and professionally affirmed sources," that the Disney Corporation and Bill Gates were collaborating on a goodwill project to fund free vacation trips to Disney World. Hardworking, worthy people who forwarded this message to at least 35 others (including the original source of the message) would supposedly receive a trip, all expenses paid—or a $1,000 check if they were unable to take their trip.

Before passing on this message, I considered checking out the authenticity of the e-mail forward. However, I didn't want to waste my valuable time checking out something I already believed to be true. So from my computer's address book, I lined up the addresses of 35 former hardworking colleagues and pushed the send button.

Two days later my face flushed crimson when I read a second e-mail from my trusted acquaintance who had sent me the earlier forward.

"Please forgive me," she began. "Someone to whom I earlier sent the Gates-Disney e-mail checked it out. He just informed me that the whole thing is a big hoax."

Believe me, missing out on an all-expense-paid trip was nothing compared to the humiliation I experienced when I had to admit to 35 hardworking acquaintances that I had not exercised my right to discern.

Exhibit C: Wilderness Photo Shoot
(Discerning Between Reality and Perception)

One Monday morning the family of a missing wildlife photographer notified our local search and rescue team. The hiker had left for a day trip into the mountains near Yosemite National Park to photograph wildflowers. Now he was one day overdue.

Within hours searchers discovered the man's parked car, unharmed, in a remote location. One team member told the others, "I'm familiar with this area. I know where tons of wildflowers grow this time of year. Maybe he hiked in that direction."

The rescue team followed this member about three miles to an alpine meadow situated atop a bluff rising steeply from the valley below. Soon they'd spotted footprints that matched those of the boots the photographer had been wearing when he left home.

"Look," said one member, "see how this young foliage is crushed—the guy's been here within the past 24 hours." The team followed the bootprints until they disappeared into a carpet of flowers between them and the nearest cliff.

One rescue worker, securing himself to a sturdy tree, leaned out over the edge of the drop-off and peered through the scraggly brush clinging to face of the cliff.

He suddenly exclaimed, "Oh, boy—we got trouble!"

"What do ya got?" another wanted to know.

"About 200 feet down—just at the base of this cliff—I see what appears to be the immobile form of a man."

At the base of the cliff a few minutes later, rescue workers found personal ID in the dead man's wallet that identified him as the missing wildlife photographer.

Amazingly, the man's camera was still intact. Investigators subsequently developed the film and shook their heads at the eerie tale it told of the photographer's demise.

The first photo had captured a multihued sea of wildflowers in the foreground with the bluff of a distant cliff in the background under a clear turquoise sky.

The next photo portrayed, from a closer vantage point, the far side of the flower patch in front of a drop-off into thin air.

The third photo revealed a close-up of isolated pink and yellow wildflowers bowing over the edge of the cliff, which projected far above a vast purplish-gray panorama.

The final photo clearly had captured the photographer's boots as they straddled some ledge-hugging wildflowers. The toes of the boots jutted into open space high above the valley below.

Unfortunately, the photographer—whether from daredevil stupidity or from an absorption in the task at hand—had not perceived the reality of his dangerous situation. This lack of discernment caused his long and lethal fall.

Exhibit D: Sidetrackers
(Discerning What's Truly Important)

Throughout His entire ministry, Christ ran across people who could not discern what was truly important in their lives and what wasn't. Not only did their lack of discernment sidetrack them, but it also distracted those around them.

Once, when Christ was methodically explaining how to discern the difference between Satan's kingdom and God's kingdom, a woman in the crowd blurted out, "Blessed is the womb that bore You, and the breasts which nursed You!" (Luke 11:27, NKJV)

Had He wanted to, Jesus could have taken advantage of this

woman's comment to praise and promote His mother. Instead He brought listeners' attention back to the main point: "More than that, blessed are those who hear the word of God and keep it!" (verse 28, NKJV)

On another occasion Christ was delivering a powerful discourse on how to be ready for—and survive—personal trials and deceptions.

A listener abruptly interrupted Him with, "Teacher, tell my brother to divide the inheritance with me" (Luke 12:13, NKJV).

Jesus answered, "Man, who made Me a judge or an arbitrator over you?" (verse 14, NKJV). Once again, Christ had to bring back the minds of His distracted listeners to the point of His message (verses 16-21).

On yet another occasion Christ was at the home of Martha. Mary, her sister, sat at Christ's feet drinking in His words. Overwhelmed by her entertaining responsibilities, Martha approached Jesus and asked, "Lord, do You not care that my sister has left me to serve alone? Therefore tell her to help me" (Luke 10:40, NKJV).

Instead Jesus said, "Martha, Martha, you are worried and troubled about many things. But one thing is needed, and Mary has chosen that good part, which will not be taken away from her" (verses 41, 42, NKJV).

As my pastor, Kevin Miller, would say, these undiscerning individuals were "letting the urgent get in the way of the important."

Only when we listen, hear, and internalize the words of Christ will we be able to discern what is truly important in our daily lives.

Exhibit E: Peter
(Discerning Between God's Better Judgment and Ours)

In the previous chapter we saw Peter having a difficult time discerning between what was best: doing things Christ's way or doing things his way. Christ simply wanted to wash the disciple's feet. Peter refused. When Christ persisted by explaining the necessity of having his feet washed, Peter then said, "Oh, OK, but wash my hands and head too!"

Peter couldn't discern the wisdom of complying with Christ's request, as he had been focusing on the temporal instead of the spiritual. Fortunately, Christ opened Peter's spiritual eyesight (John 13:12-17).

"Getting" Discernment

How do we become discerning?

First of all, discernment takes *time*—time with God. Our heavenly Father says, "Be still and know that I am God" (Ps. 46:10). Being still—to reflect and evaluate details within the big picture—takes time. If I had taken the *time* to check out that e-mail forward, I would have discerned how preposterous it was, as well as saving myself embarrassment and time. Taking time with God eventually *saves* us time—and embarrassment.

Second, discernment takes *effort*. That's what King David was sharing with his heir, Solomon, when he said, "Now set your heart and your soul to *seek* the Lord your God" (1 Chron. 22:19).

For most of us, discernment doesn't just happen. If the mountain fisherman had made the *effort* to purchase a compass—and consult it—he would have discerned true north and not gotten lost. He would have discovered where he actually was instead of where he *thought* he was. But he didn't make the effort, and lost his way.

Finally, discernment requires *information*. The Bible states that "wise people store up knowledge" (Prov. 10:14, NKJV). If the photographer had stopped looking into the camera lens and looked for his bearings instead, he would have had enough information to act on his reality instead of on his perceptions. His lack of information regarding imminent danger led to a tragic lack of discernment.

Information—true knowledge—comes only from God. That's why it's so essential that we not give the Word just a cursory reading each day. It's just as important to ask for the Spirit's guidance while we study God's Word as it is to read it.

Jesus referred to the Holy Spirit as "the Spirit of truth; whom the world cannot receive, because it seeth him not, neither knoweth him: but ye know him; for he dwelleth with you, and shall be in you" (John 14:17). A few breaths later Christ added that the Holy Spirit "will teach you all things" (verse 26).

As we've mentioned earlier, spending time in the Word—under

the Holy Spirit's guidance—will lead us to know and love God more.

Spending time in the Word will also lead us to a love of the truth. And this truth will enable us to be balanced in discernment—no matter what appearances may suggest.

HOMEWORK FOR THE HEART

Prayer for Discernment. I most often feel the need of discernment when having to make difficult decisions. I suspect that you, right now, may have at least one situation in your life for which you covet God's discernment.

God has promised to give us wisdom when we ask for it. So why not ask Him right now for wisdom concerning your situation and then continue making it a matter of ongoing prayer? (Write out your prayer, then date it. How exciting it will be to see how God leads in this matter!)

Reminder: Exercising our right to discern requires time, effort, and a knowledge that only God can give.

⋆ E. C. McKenzie, *14,000 Quips and Quotes*, p. 277.

▲

CHAPTER 20

POISON OAK

OUR RIGHT TO RECEIVE A LOVE OF THE TRUTH

"They received not the love of the truth, that they might be saved."
—*The apostle Paul*[1]

*"And I will pray the Father, and he shall give you
another Comforter . . . even the Spirit of truth."*
—*Jesus*[2]

"Truth often hurts, but it's the lie that leaves the scars."[3]

WHEN SOUTHERN OREGON WEATHER PERMITS, I love to take early morning walks in the little woods behind our house—especially in the springtime. Tender-tipped new evergreen growth brushes my head at every turn in the trail.

Baby lime-green shrubs push their way up through the yellow-and-lavender dappled carpet of spring flowers. I observe history in the making. For this morning's baby shrubs are tomorrow's mighty oaks that will one day shade weary hikers, feed hungry squirrels, and shelter squawking bluejays.

Tucked amid all this new-growth beauty grows another new plant, nearly identical in appearance to the oak shrub. Yet, during its lifetime, it will never serve any worthy purpose. And any creature brushing against its red-tinged leaves will carry away an imperceptible streak of rash-inducing oil.

Only a discerning eye can distinguish the difference between an incipient young oak and its toxic look-alike, poison oak. In fact, the only way I can tell the difference between the two is that I know what real oak leaves look like. Only after comparing a shrub's leaf with what I know to be the real thing can I identify the counterfeit from the true.

Fresh Advice From an Old Source

On a recent airplane trip, I noticed the passenger in the seat ahead of me reading *The Wall Street Journal*. One subhead identified an article on that page as a book review for a new tome about how to make safe investments in financially shaky times. The article's title promised, "Sound Advice for Scary Times."

I couldn't help recalling another book chock-full of sound advice for these scary times: the Holy Bible. As we've affirmed again and again in this book, the Bible offers invaluable advice for how to stay spiritually balanced during these times in which we live. Yet it also prepares us for something most of us don't care to think about because it's too disturbing. That is a great end-time deception.

Several weeks ago my doctor did some medical tests and sadly shared with me the results as well as his medical diagnosis. I have breast cancer.

Now, if I didn't want the cancer to destroy me, I had to make some choices—and fast. I hated being caught up in a process that I would *never* have chosen! Yet I had to make choices (starting with surgery) or else the cancer would make choices for me.

When I start aggressive treatment, I will not be able to turn back. I don't look forward to treatment that may result in a great deal of physical discomfort. Yet, what would make me want to return to my previous status quo: a pain-free body insidiously being consumed by cancer? Like it or not, I'm part of a situation not of my own choosing.

Likewise, by simply being born into this world, we were automatically caught up in a situation not of our own choosing. Our birth on Planet Earth simply dumped us into the midst of a fast-growing cancer: sin. Sin is propelling us—on a very fast track—to earth's final cataclysmic events, when God will put an end to this disease. Current events and Bible prophecy, being fulfilled daily, point to the fact that we are indeed living in the time of the end.

Bible characters prophesied about an end-time period in which "times and laws" would be changed (Dan. 7:25); "the truth of God" would be changed "into a lie" (Rom. 1:25); and, if possible, even "the very elect"—as Jesus Himself put it—would be deceived (Matt. 24:24).

Paul specifically stated that, spiritually speaking, those not being able to tell the real thing from "poison oak" would be individuals who "received not the love of the truth, that they might be saved" (2 Thess. 2:10).

So what exactly is this "truth" that God calls us to love and that will help enable our salvation?

In the upper room, Christ shared with His disciples the essence of how to "love" the truth when He said, "I am the way, the *truth,* and the life" (John 14:6). He was inviting them (and us) into a saving relationship with Himself.

Later that evening, in the Garden of Gethsemane, Christ's words to His Father were reminiscent of David's earlier thoughts when he wrote, "Thy law is the truth" (Ps. 119:142; also see verse 151). On His knees just hours before the Crucifixion Jesus prayerfully acknowledged, "Thy word is truth" (John 17:17).

The Ways of Deception

If we are not "watchful," as Jesus asked us to be, then even those of us who have embraced truth, both in a relationship with Christ and in the Word of God, can still be deceived in a number of ways.

First of all, what another person says or does can distract us *from* what we know to be true. And then we start to forget to remember what the truth actually is.

One summer evening I sat behind a young man at an outdoor camp meeting service. The young man sported scruffy blond dreadlocks several inches in length. Whenever he moved his head they quivered stiffly, brushing his shoulders. Pieces of dandruff at their base suggested he hadn't recently washed his hair.

Intermittently he scratched the crown of his head with his right hand. Then he slipped the fingers of his left hand up under the tangle of hair at the nape of his neck in order to scratch that part of his scalp.

I tried to ignore him and keep my focus on the message of the evening speaker. Soon, however, the crown of my head began to itch. A sudden pinpoint sensation (could it be a tiny insect?) twinged at the nape of my neck. I felt another twinge on my temple just above my right ear.

The fingers of my left hand made their way to the back of my neck and discreetly massaged the irritating spot. Suddenly my whole scalp felt itchy and grimy.

Oh, dear, I wondered, *when did I shampoo last?* Then I recalled I'd shampooed within two hours of coming to this very meeting. My hair and scalp were still squeaky clean. Yet the behavior of the young man in front of me had distracted me from what I knew to be reality, and I'd forgotten about the truth of the matter.

Disappearance

Another way we can lose our love of the truth (as well as our spiritual balance) is to not value—and guard—the truth we already have.

I once attended a conference in Berkeley, California. One afternoon, during a long break between meetings, I came back to my hotel room to rest. Kicking off my shoes, I turned down one side of the bed's comforter before repositioning two of the three pillows for a backrest. I leaned against them, put my feet up on the bed, and read over some of the conference handouts.

Wanting diversion a bit later, I made a quick trip to the downstairs lobby for that day's newspaper.

Back in my room, I realized I needed to leave soon for the early evening session. First, I would grab a quick bite somewhere before returning to the conference site. I slipped on my shoes, touched up my hair, and looked for my purse.

I couldn't find it.

Quickly I searched all surfaces—chairs, the table, the foot of the bed, dresser tops, nightstands, the bathroom counter, and even the floor under the bed.

Still no purse. My body went cold.

That black leather purse contained *everything* I needed for safety and independence that weekend—money, credit cards, checkbook, health information, and car keys.

"Where's my purse?" I asked out loud again and again. "I've had it with me all day. I got my room key out of it when I came back to the hotel. So it *has* to be here!" But clearly it wasn't.

The only time I'd been separated from my purse was that five-minute period when I'd gone to the lobby for a newspaper.

Obviously someone had taken advantage of my short absence and robbed me! I felt duped, violated, and helpless.

At least I still had my room key! In a daze, I hurried downstairs to the lobby to report the theft (suspiciously eyeing a couple of cleaning ladies en route).

Color drained from the face of the hotel manager when I told him about my missing purse. He motioned for me to step around the side of the front desk. After asking a few questions, he requested I not say anything to any one else while he notified the police from a distant phone.

He returned. "The police are on their way to interview you and search the hotel." He leaned over the desk and spoke in hushed tones. "Look, I know you don't have any money right now so please be my guest for dinner. Order anything off the menu—and as much as you want. I'll alert the maître dˇ you're coming after the police have a chance to talk to you."

Ten minutes later a police officer interviewed me in my hotel room and made a list of my purse's contents. "Chances of recovering your purse in a city like this are very slim," he pointed out. "But just in case, my fellow officers are checking out all the hotel landings right now. A couple of them are on the roof even as we speak."

The officer thoroughly checked out my room window as a possible entrance site and any other possible areas that would provide clues concerning the alleged burglar. Then he left, promising to phone should my purse show up.

I couldn't drive to my conference that evening because I didn't have any car keys. I couldn't call a cab because I had no money. At least I might as well eat as the guest of the hotel manager.

Faulty Conclusion

I went downstairs to the hotel dining room. Obviously the hotel manager had instructed the waiters to treat me right so I'd keep mum about the purloined purse. They nearly fell over one another rushing the various courses of my meal to the table.

Despondent and back in my hotel room, I decided to turn in early. Exhausted from my ordeal, I pushed aside the top pillow, which I'd been using as part of the improvised backrest for my afternoon's reading.

Sandwiched in between the two remaining pillows was my missing black leather purse!

I gasped.

Not even the police officer had discovered it when hastily searching my room! I realized that discovering the truth about my purse had set me free. Once again I had ID cards, money, and car keys. I could pay my hotel bill and be free to leave the next morning. Quickly I phoned the police department.

Then, shamefaced, I carried my purse into the hotel lobby and apologized to the manager. His facial muscles visibly relaxed at the news. When I offered to reimburse him for my dinner, he politely (if not coolly) refused.

I trudged back up the stairs toward my room, shaking my head. "That 'stolen' purse—with its all-important contents—had been only an arm's length away all afternoon," I told myself. "How could I possibly have missed it?"

The answer was simple.

I'd been careless with my purse. I'd not really valued it enough to notice where I'd dropped it. When I needed it, I couldn't find it—in a frantic, cursory search anyway. Then, when I couldn't find it again, I believed logical, but faulty, "evidence." Faulty evidence always leads to a faulty conclusion. In my self-deception, I also deceived the hotel manager as well as the entire Berkeley Police Department!

Loving It

After such a scare, I can't tell you how much I have grown to value my purse, if not downright *love* it! I can't tell you how important it is for me to know where it is at all times. If I know where my purse is, I also know where my checkbook is . . . and my car keys . . . and my credit cards . . . and my weekly calendar. I live life with so much more confidence and efficiency when I have the security of my purse and its contents.

It's the same with truth. If we value and love the truth—as God would have us experience it through His Son and in His Word—

our spiritual walk will be much more confident and efficient. On the other hand, if we don't value—and guard—the truth, we will eventually lose sight of it and lose our balance in the process.

I still marvel that neither the interrogating police officer that afternoon nor I uncovered the purse during our respective searches. Looking back, however, I realize we didn't find it because we were both in too much of a hurry.

Diligent searching for a purse takes time.

Diligent searching for Christ-centered, end-time truth also takes time. It takes time for a lasting, loving relationship to develop. We fall in love with truth the same way we fall in love with a person—by spending time with it, by experiencing its redemptive, rejuvenating influence in our daily lives.

When we are familiar with the real thing, we won't be deceived or injured by the "poison oak" of deception. We will know the truth—and love it. After all, that's our right.

HOMEWORK FOR THE HEART

Opening Up. How can I be more open to receiving a love of the truth?

"Dear Lord, please show me how to be more open to receiving a love of Your truth. I never want to lose sight of You or Your precious Word. I don't want to be deceived. Amen."

Reminder: Loving and accepting God's Son and His Word keep end-time deceptions from seducing us.

---

[1] 2 Thess. 2:10.
[2] John 14:16, 17.
[3] E. C. McKenzie, *14,000 Quips and Quotes,* p. 521.

CHAPTER 21

▲

CRACKING THE CASE OF THE PROPHETIC DREAM

OUR RIGHT TO APPLY THE TRUTH

"Don't let your faith become unbalanced by every kind of strange doctrine that comes along. May your hearts be strengthened by God's grace."
—Paul to the Hebrews[1]

"And ye shall know the truth, and the truth shall make you free."
—Jesus to His disciples[2]

TIME AFTER TIME THE BIBLE WARNS US about end-time deceptions throwing us off balance. Paul forewarned the Thessalonians to be on the alert, "That ye be not soon shaken in mind, or be troubled, neither by spirit, nor by word, . . . as that the day of Christ is at hand. Let no man deceive you by any means" (2 Thess. 2:2, 3).

Jesus warned against extremely convincing false prophets, false christs, signs, and wonders (Matt. 24:24).

An astounding article in a respected religious magazine reveals how New Age philosophies have gained not only acceptance—but also respect and inclusion—in the corporate world.

The article states that more than 500 businesspersons recently attended a conference organized by entities "unifying the disciples and doctrines of a constellation of neopagan and panreligious philosophers, metaphysical futurists, and self-proclaimed gurus who recognize the power of business in today's society."[3]

One doesn't have to attend a big conference to be exposed to blowing "winds of doctrine." You've probably noticed that in almost any mainstream bookstore, pantheism, New Age philosophies, Eastern religions, and exotic philosophies (old and new) quietly infuse the majority of books in the "Self-Help" and "Spirituality" sections.

Since the time of Christ, strange "winds of doctrine" have continued gathering momentum. Today they swirl across our planet, touching down like tornadoes that suck the naive and unwary up into their deadly vortexes.

Negotiating one's way through these subtle, often seductive, philosophies can be a bit like balancing on a tightrope. Tightrope walkers on a high wire carry a long pole whose ends they dip and raise to ensure both balance and safety. We too need a balance pole.

For the Christian this balance pole is the truth of God's truth—applied to daily situations. Applying God's truth to our daily lives is yet another right He grants us to exercise in His name.

Though I am still in the better-balance learning curve, I'm so grateful for the more spiritually experienced "tightrope walkers" whom God has placed in my life at critical times. When I needed them most, they walked out onto the tightrope with me, steadying my "pole" by applying God's truth to my situations.

Though many years have passed, I still refer to one of these times as "Cracking the Case of the Prophetic Dream."

Mrs. G's Prophetic Dream

Before sunup one morning, on an African mission where I lived, my husband and 5-year-old son departed with the chauffeur of the mission truck for the capital city. They planned to bring home the big wooden crates bearing our clothes and living supplies, which we'd shipped from the U.S. during our recent furlough.

Around breakfasttime a fellow missionary pounded at my front door. Mrs. G (as I will call her, since I've long forgotten her name) was a retired short-term volunteer missionary in her late 60s. For a few weeks she and her husband were overseeing the building of some new classrooms. I was not well acquainted with them.

Mrs. G was almost hyperventilating and fidgeting with the collar of her blouse. I invited her in and sat down on the couch beside her.

"Is your little boy all right today?" she anxiously inquired.

"I think so," I answered. "He's with his father."

"Oh, good!" she sighed, extending her head toward the hallways, as if she assumed they were both in another room. "Just don't let that darling child out of your sight today."

"Oh, it's too late for that," I chuckled. "He and his father are on their way to the capital.

"Oh, no!" she exclaimed. "It is probably too late—too late."

"Mrs. G," I asked in alarm, "what is it?"

She swallowed hard. "I don't know how to break this to you," she almost moaned. "But I was shown in a dream last night that your son will likely be killed today. I didn't want to come too early and wake you up. But I wanted to come in time to warn you. Now it may be too late!"

The palms of my hands grew clammy.

"Oh, my dear," she said sympathetically, as if comforting someone who had just lost a loved one, "I have a history of dreams from the Lord. Once I dreamed my son would get caught in barbed wire. The next day he did. Then I dreamed my husband would have an auto accident and he did, but survived. And there are lots of other times I could tell you about.

"So now when I have a prophetic dream like this, I warn people so that they can perhaps avoid the specified danger. But in your case . . . " She bit her lower lip and shook her head.

Fearfully I asked, "What *exactly* did you see in your dream?"

"First of all," she said, "I heard a distinct male voice that kept saying, 'The Rathburn boy is dead! The Rathburn boy is dead!' Then I saw a little blond boy running around in a dark place—sort of like a warehouse. Then I saw something like a huge wooden crate beginning to fall down toward him. But I didn't see what happened."

A dry knot choked my throat.

Mrs. G continued, "Oh, I hope the dream doesn't come true! Here, let me pray with you—that God will prepare you for the worst."

She prayed a short prayer and then left to rejoin her husband for their day's work.

Applying the Truth

Sensations of stifling panic squeezed the breath from my chest.

God, I silently implored, *was that dream really from You?*

I had to talk to somebody!

I hurried across the little dirt road to the school principal's house.

His wife was home. She was older than I and a woman of prayer. Cordially she ushered me in.

By now I was crying, but managed to explain what troubled me. "Oh, please, *please* pray with me for my son's protection," I implored.

Calmly the principal's wife sat me down and said, "Of course I will pray with you. But first I want to tell you something."

Simply and clearly she began exercising her right to apply God's truth to my situation.

"You know me well enough by now to know I don't gossip," she began.

I nodded my head, for she was right.

"But in this case," she continued, "and for your peace of mind I'm going to tell you something without going into details. The Bible says one sign for distinguishing a true prophet from a false one is behavior. 'By their fruits you shall know them.'[4] Ever since Mrs. G arrived, she has been manifesting some very un-Christlike 'fruits.' She has offended many of the African workers and seems to spend much of her time complaining and criticizing."

I watched the director's wife struggling through her uncharacteristically pointed remarks.

"Because of Mrs. G's erratic and critical witness," she concluded, "I strongly doubt God would use her as His consistent mouthpiece to fellow believers. That being said, let's pray for your little boy."

Then she quietly took my hands and prayed with me.

Somewhat reassured, I returned home.

Later that day, when my next-door neighbor returned from teaching, I hurried to her house. Since she was also a woman of prayer, I wanted to ask for her prayers of protection for my son as well.

Quietly she listened. When I got to the place in the story where Mrs. G described a distinct male voice declaring 'The Rathburn boy is dead!' my neighbor stopped me.

"Wait a minute," she said. "Who was she talking about?"

"About our son!" I said, wondering why she was suddenly having trouble tracking.

"Do you believe that God knows the numbers of the hairs on your head, as He has claimed?" she asked (see Matt. 10:30).

"Yes," I responded.

"Do you believe that He has known you as well as your son since before either of you were born, as Psalm 139 tells us?"

Again I nodded.

"All right, then, the voice in Mrs. G's dream said that the Rath-*burn* boy is dead. Your last name isn't Rath-*burn*," she emphasized the last syllable. "It's Rath-*bun*.

"Come on, Carolyn," she said, "don't you think the good Lord knows you well enough to at least get your last name right?" With a sympathetic smile she said, "Now let's pray."

For the first time that day I experienced complete peace.

About 10:00 that night the school truck rolled in with my husband, my very-much-alive little boy, and our previously shipped crates. My family members had not been in any type of warehouse that day, and all little Kent could talk about were the toys he remembered packing in the crates before we shipped them from the States.

I don't believe for a moment that Mrs. G was purposely trying to deceive me. And she probably *did* have the dream she described. Yet my response to it did not have to be her response. My two truth-based neighbors gently reminded me that I must always look at the bigger picture if I don't want to be unnecessarily troubled, at the least, or misled, at the worst.

The facilitator of a weekly Bible study we attend helps keep us biblically accountable. If someone pipes up with "Well, the Bible says . . . " the facilitator always responds with "Give me a text." We need those timely reminders.

Christ in the Wilderness

In an earlier chapter we briefly discussed Christ's temptation in the wilderness and the importance of resisting the enemy of our souls.

In the wilderness Christ experienced attempted deception at its most subtle. He met it head on by exercising His right to *apply* the truth—God's Word—to His situations of temptation.

After Christ had fasted 40 days the enemy appeared to Him. Don't you think that if the enemy was coming to Christ in the guise of a comforter, he would present himself as an "angel of light"

(2 Cor. 11:14)? What a reminder *that we cannot rely solely upon our senses in this day and age.* Strange and unusual events are occurring in both the secular and religious world.

The enemy tempted and taunted Christ, saying that *if* He were really the Son of God, He could certainly command the stones about His feet to become loaves of bread. As with the serpent in the Garden of Eden, the temper's words once again betrayed his true character as he attempted to introduce doubt into the Lord's mind about the reality of His heavenly Sonship.

Christ answered with Scripture: "It is written, That man shall not live by bread alone, but by every word of God" (Luke 4:4).

Again the enemy approached, offering Christ dominion over the kingdoms of the world if He would worship Satan.

As with the first temptation, Jesus applied the truth, rebuking the tempter. "Get thee behind me, Satan: for it is written, Thou shalt worship the Lord thy God, and him only shalt thou serve" (Luke 4:8).

With the final wilderness temptation, Satan also *appeared* to apply God's truth to Christ's situation. After once again openly questioning Christ's divine Sonship, he too said, "For it is written" (verse 10).

One final time his words betray him as an enemy, for he quotes *only a part* of the scriptural passage, suggesting that Jesus should presumptuously risk His life (jump off the pinnacle of the Temple) to prove a point to His accuser.

And one final time, Christ applies God's Word—relying on its truth—in order to unmask the enemy's attempted deception: "It is said, Thou shalt not tempt the Lord" (verse 12).

If God's own Son used His Father's Word to resist and unmask deceivers and attempted deception, should we think we can do otherwise and still be spiritually safe?

Being Set Free

Our right to apply the truth to uncertain spiritual issues brings us back to the importance of knowing God's Word. Not only is it the strength behind our ability to resist spiritual imbalance in our lives, but it is the "balance pole" that keeps us walking on the tightrope.

In the Temple one day Jesus said, "And ye shall know the truth, and the truth shall make you free" (John 8:32). That's what the truth did for me when my two neighbors applied God's Word to the frightful scenario Mrs. G presented to me so long ago. The truth set me free from disabling fear and also helped me realize Mrs. G's dreams weren't necessarily prophetic ones.

God wants us to exercise our right to apply His truth to everyday "tightrope" situations so that we will walk with increasing balance.

HOMEWORK FOR THE HEART

Brushing Up on the Truth. Should you ever wonder about the validity of an unfamiliar doctrine or philosophy; should you ever want to evaluate a rational-sounding pitch by the latest television talk-show guru or even an old idea with a new twist being pushed by an apparent Christian, apply the following truths. (It's your right!) Whatever you are evaluating must pass muster with *all* of them.

Truth 1: Even if a person claims to speak in God's name, a prophecy often won't come to pass if it is spoken on the prophet's authority—not God's (Deut. 18:21, 22; see also Jer. 28:9). However, bear in mind that the enemy can also work miracles (2 Thess. 2:9, 10).

Truth 2: If the prophet uses prophecies, signs, and wonders to draw others away from biblical teaching to different philosophies, he/she is speaking falsely (Deut. 13:1-3).

Truth 3: If prophecies, dreams, and visions don't agree with the law and the prophets (the Bible), they aren't of God (Isa. 8:19, 20).

Truth 4: If a message or messenger is not *Christ-centered,* don't fall for either. Revelation 12:17 and 19:10 define "spirit of prophecy" as the "testimony of Jesus" (1 John 4:1-3).

Truth 5: The lifestyle of a true prophet will be pure, manifesting choices that are consistent with biblical requirements. A false prophet's behavior will eventually reveal the opposite (Matt. 7:18, 20). In Galatians 5 Paul contrasted the fruits of the Spirit (verses 22 and 23) with the works of darkness (verses 19-21).

Applying the Truth. From what sources am I most likely to be influenced by ideas, beliefs, or doctrines that are not truth, when placed in the light of God's Word?

What can I do to protect myself from being influenced by these sources?

Reminder: Familiarity with God's Word sharpens our awareness of— and provides a defense against—enemy deceptions.

---

[1] Heb. 13:9, Clear Word.

[2] John 8:32.

[3] Jeff M. Sellers, "The Higher Self Gets Down to Business (An Old Movement Appears Anew—in the Corporate World)," *Christianity Today,* February 2003, p. 34.

[4] Matt. 7:20.

▲

CHAPTER 22

NURTURING THE EVIL 5 PERCENT, OR EMBRACING THE LIGHT?

OUR RIGHT TO BE HOLY

"Be ye holy; for I am holy."
—God, as quoted by Peter[1]

"Virtue has more admirers than followers."
—Unknown[2]

A JUNIOR HIGH STUDENT OF MINE once confided that he had started a home business.

"Really?" I responded, pleased this young man was showing entrepreneurial aspirations at such an early age.

"And what is your business?" I asked.

"I have a worm farm."

"I beg your pardon? A worm farm? I've never heard of such a thing. What is it?"

"I am growing worms to sell to fishermen in this area. In case you're interested, I'll cut you a special deal—as long as you buy at least a dozen. I have a lot of worms already."

"Where do you grow your worms?" I asked. "Do you have some type of dirt-filled box in your backyard that you keep damp for them?"

"No," he explained. "I grow them in my bedroom—in the bottom drawer of my dresser."

"In your dresser drawer!" I blinked hard. "What does your mother think about your business?"

"I don't know," he said, shrugging his shoulders. "I haven't told her about it yet."

Do you and I have any worms growing in the dark, dirty corners of our spiritual dresser drawers?

I used to think that if I was doing the "right things" 95 percent of the time, an occasional indulgence of something less than holy couldn't really hurt me. Things such as an occasional R-rated video, if I sort of averted my eyes when the R parts rolled across the screen.

Then I began to notice that the evil 5 percent always surfaced at the most unexpected times—whether it was impure images stored in my brain, a consistently unhealthful dietary choice, or the indulgence of a negative habit such as procrastination. One can't ever predict when that evil 5 percent will attack.

Jimbo's Evil 5 Percent

"This is Jimbo," said a friend when her black cat came into her living room (I've changed the cat's name to ensure his privacy).

The cat paused beside my left ankle, lowered its head, and leaned into my shin. He rubbed his head back and forth against my lower pants leg as my friend and I continued visiting.

"What a pretty boy you are!" I said to the cat during a break in the conversation. Jimbo raised his head so I could scratch him under the chin.

"He's a really sweet cat," said my friend, "except for about 5 percent. We call it his 'evil 5 percent.' So be careful."

Instinctively I withdrew my hand. The big black cat stared back at me with winsome yellow eyes. Then he gracefully leaped into my lap, where he sank down, purring loudly.

"Hey, big guy," I cooed, beginning to stroke his head and shoulders. Jimbo closed his eyes in ecstasy.

Surprise Attack

I was in midsentence when the deceptively contented bundle of black fur in my lap exploded.

A sudden hiss! A yowl of unprovoked rage!

Startled, I jerked my hands away. Jimbo dove to the floor and headed for the front door.

"Bad kitty!" exclaimed my friend, opening the front door. The cat shot across the threshold.

I made a feeble attempt at humor. "Was it something I said?" My voice, however, sounded unconvincing. Four deep and perfectly spaced tooth punctures in my left hand were beginning to bleed.

Nervously dabbing at my bite wounds with a tissue, I asked, "May I wash my hand?"

My friend and I finished visiting before she accompanied me to my car. Jimbo was waiting for me on the hood. As I approached he began purring loudly and stretched his neck toward me, begging to be petted.

"You must think I'm dumber than I look!" I said to him before opening the car door. Jimbo jumped down and disappeared around the corner of the garage.

On the way home I reflected on the elegant black cat with the ready purr and the endearing behavior. He was perfect—except for that little 5 percent. He so much reminded me of, well, of me.

My Evil 5 Percent—And Yours

All too often—just when I think I'm getting the hang of being spiritually balanced—my evil 5 percent suddenly comes to life. I am living proof (perhaps you are too) of Jeremiah's words: "The heart is deceitful above all things, and desperately wicked; who can know it?" His next words provide the answer: "I, the Lord, search the heart, I test the mind" (Jer. 17:9, 10, NKJV).

Peter and Christ demonstrated the truthfulness of this text that evening in the upper room. Peter *looked* like a follower of Christ and even *sounded* like one. "I will lay down my life for thy sake," he proclaimed to Christ in front of all the other disciples (John 13:37). Yet in Christ's very next breath He prophesied that Peter's evil 5 percent would surface three times before daybreak. And it did.

After the Resurrection and before He returned to heaven, Jesus asked Peter three times—in a roundabout way—if he would be purged of his evil 5 percent (John 21:15-19). Christ's specific question was "Do you *love* Me?" In other words, do you love Me enough to do what I might ask you to do? Peter said yes (verses 15-17).

After Christ's ascension those around Peter marveled at his continuing growth in spiritual balance and holiness. His evil 5 percent surfaced less frequently than it had before. Moreover, when he spoke, listeners recognized in his words and behavior (along with John's) that he had been with Jesus (Acts 4:13).

The more Peter allowed the Holy Spirit to steady him on the balance beam, the more he resembled Christ. Peter came to understand that it was not only his God-given right to be 100 percent holy but also his God-requested obligation. Peter is the apostle who recalled God's words from the Old Testament, "Be ye holy; for I am holy" (1 Peter 1:16).

When Isaiah saw God in vision, he fell on his face and exclaimed, "Holy, holy, holy, is the Lord of hosts" (Isa. 6:3).

In his book *The Holiness of God* R. C. Sproul points out that we never read a Bible verse that states God is just, just, just. Or that He is love, love, love. Yet He *is* "holy, holy, holy" (Isa. 6:3).

Many people define holiness as simple purity. Yet the Bible uses the word "holy" to call attention to *everything* that God is. "It reminds us that His love is *holy* love, His justice is *holy* justice, His mercy is *holy* mercy . . . His spirit is the holy Spirit."[3]

At a camp meeting I once heard speaker Roy Gane of Andrews University describe holiness as the sum of God's attributes.[4]

Perhaps Paul's later interaction with Peter prompted the reformed persecutor to write, "Having therefore these promises, dearly beloved, let us cleanse ourselves from all filthiness of the flesh and spirit, perfecting holiness in the fear of God" (2 Cor. 7:1).

God reminds us that He hasn't called us to be unclean but rather He has called us to "holiness" (1 Thess. 4:7).

I don't know about you, but when I catch clearer glimpses of who God is—through His Word, during sermons, in the lives of godly people around me, or while I'm at prayer—I *also* catch clearer glimpses of who I am. And it's not a very pretty picture. In fact, holiness seems so unattainable in a sin-filled world. Many of us aren't even sure what it is.

That's why I appreciate this simple definition of holiness: "Holiness is agreement with God."[5]

How can a person be in "agreement with God"?

A Threefold Gift

Tucked away in the obscure Old Testament book of Zechariah, chapter 3, is a wonderful little four-verse story that simply and clearly lays out the answer to this question.

Let's first "set up" this story, as I used to do for my students before we would read one from our textbook.

Main Characters

The angel

The angel in this story—as distinguished from the other heavenly beings present—is rendered in earlier translations as "the angel of the Lord" or "the angel who is the Lord." In other words, Christ.

Joshua

Joshua (or Jeshua, which was the name of the first high priest after the Captivity) represents you and me, for we are also called to be priests (see Rev. 1:6).

The plot

The plot simply portrays how Joshua became holy (in other words, how you and I can become holy).

Let's read this beautiful little story.

Verse 3 (NIV): "Now Joshua was dressed in filthy clothes [representing unholiness] as he stood before the angel."

Verse 4: "The angel said to those who were standing before him, 'Take off his filthy clothes' [God's forgiveness of our sins—whatever they have been or may be in the present, if we repent and confess them].

"Then he said to Joshua [as Christ also speaks to us], 'See, I have taken away your sin, and I will put rich garments on you.'"[6] (Notice that the old garments aren't simply covered up or glossed over. Jesus transfers them to Himself and suffers the penalty for wearing our filthiness. In their place, He promises to cover us with the rich garments of His imputed character.)

Verse 5: "Then I said, 'Put a clean turban on his head.' So they put a clean turban on his head [you may recall that the turban, or mitre of Israel's high priest, also carried these words, "Holiness to the Lord"] and clothed him, while the angel of the Lord stood by [justification, for after this divine transaction, God views us as holy because Christ has covered us with His righteousness]."

Verses 6 and 7: "The angel of the Lord gave this charge to Joshua: 'This is what the Lord Almighty says: "If you will walk in my ways [being in "constant agreement" with God through obedience to His Word] and keep my requirements [growth in sanctification or increasing holiness], then you will govern my house and have charge of my courts, and I will give you a place among these standing here"'" (Zech. 3:3-7, NIV).

That is glorification (Rom. 8:17, 18)—the dazzling, eternal outcome of justification and sanctification having done their perfect work in us. Imagine living in the presence of God's glory throughout eternity—because of what Christ has done for us!

Let's take one final glance at the three main components of this story—and of what Christ wants to do for us.

Justification is a gift of grace, an instantaneous act of God in response to our repentance and confession of sins.

Sanctification, continuing growth in holiness, occurs by God's grace as well and becomes more and more apparent by our joyful obedience. Paul tells us that Jesus walked the path of obedience before us. "Though he were a Son, yet learned he obedience by the things which he suffered; and being made perfect, he became the author of eternal salvation unto all them that obey him" (Heb. 5:8, 9).

Glorification is the final, humanly indescribable gift God bestows on us as He welcomes us into eternity (Rom 8:30; 1 Cor. 15:51-53).

How amazing that God doesn't ask us to *generate* our own obedience! His grace *enables* it! (Rom. 1:5). God has promised to put His will into our minds and even write it on our hearts (Heb. 8:10). Of His own obedience Christ said, "I seek not mine own will, but the will of the Father which hath sent me" (John 5:30).

Someone once wrote that obedience is renouncing our sins—when we come to recognize them as such—and then embracing the light of God's will as it shines on our pathway. I like that. I like thinking of obedience as "embracing the light" of God's desires for me.

Blessings in the Embrace

When we walk forward on the balance beam, embracing the light God gives us, what blessings are ours!

For starters, God has promised the *Holy Spirit* to anyone who obeys Him (Acts 5:32). This Comforter will give us wisdom for our perilous journey.

Furthermore, to anyone who loves God through obedience (John 14:15), *Christ promises to reveal Himself* (verse 21)! And He does, often in ways that astonish, touch, and reassure us of His care.

Finally, Christ promises that both *He and the Father will take up residence* in any obedient heart (verse 23).

The Obedient Heart

Obedient hearts usually follow in the wake of obedient thoughts.

Not long ago my husband and I spent four weeks in El Salvador on a mission trip.

One morning our host wanted to take us to an open market. On our way the two cars directly in front of ours suddenly screeched to a halt, tires laying lines of rubber on the pavement. Our host also hit his brakes with such force that our heads jerked forward and then backward against our seats.

As traffic again advanced we saw the reason for this sudden stop. Three armed military personnel, on a nearby street corner, were pointing their rifles at two men in civilian clothes.

The two men, rather than standing upright, were spread-eagled facedown across the curb, feet in the gutter and torsos on the sidewalk. The soldiers were frisking the detainees with handheld metal detectors.

As these soldiers did, we should also do. We should "frisk" every attitude, word, and projected act in our lives in the light of Paul's sin detector: Philippians 4:8. The message of this verse is "Stop sin at the thought level!"

Paul himself chose to bring "into captivity every thought to the obedience of Christ" (2 Cor. 10:5).

Speaking of stopping sin at the thought level, have you seen any soap operas lately? One radio pastor quipped that if soap writers took immorality out of the soaps, the only thing left would be the advertisements!

The radio pastor went on to remind his listeners that Joseph didn't hang around Potiphar's wife long enough to fight lust. Rather, he dropped whatever he had to (including his cloak, which she was grasping) and *fled* lust. Both Paul and Timothy tell us to flee lust (1 Cor. 6:18; 2 Tim. 2:22).

Back to Peter

Peter, who well knew the challenge of walking life's balance beam in holiness, gave us another strategy for "embracing the light." He told us to focus on God's promises. He reminds us that we have been given "exceeding great and precious promises: that by these ye might be partakers of the divine nature, having escaped the corruption that is in the world through lust" (2 Peter 1:4).

Again, Paul backs up Peter with the same message to us: "Having therefore these promises, dearly beloved, let us cleanse ourselves from all filthiness of the flesh and spirit, perfecting holiness in the fear of God" (2 Cor. 7:1).

Is it possible to truly gain the victory over that evil 5 percent in our lives? Yes, through God's strength and provisions, it is!

"Be ye holy." This is Christ's mandate to us. It is also our God-given right!

HOMEWORK FOR THE HEART

Help for Holiness. After meditating on the following quotes, ask yourself how you can apply these incredible realities to your own evil 5 percent.

Meditation 1. "Those who consecrate body, soul, and spirit to God, will constantly receive a new endowment of physical, mental, and spiritual power. The inexhaustible supplies of heaven are at their command. Christ gives them the breath of His own Spirit, the life of His own life. The Holy Spirit puts forth His highest energies to work in heart and mind. The grace of God enlarges and multiplies their faculties, and every perfection of the divine nature comes to their assistance in the work of saving souls. Through cooperation with Christ, they are made complete in Him, and in their human weakness they are enabled to do the deeds of Omnipotence."[7]

Meditation 2. "All that Christ received from God we too may have. Then ask and receive. With the persevering faith of Jacob, with the unyielding persistence of Elijah, claim for yourself all that God has promised."[8]

Reminder: Growing holiness in our lives is possible through God's provisions of justification (by grace through faith) and sanctification (as manifested in our willing obedience to "embrace the light" of God's revealed will).

---

[1] 1 Peter 1:16.

[2] E. C. McKenzie, *14,000 Quips and Quotes,* p. 534.

[3] R. C. Sproul, *The Holiness of God* (Wheaton, Ill.: Tyndale House Publishers, 1998), p. 40.

[4] You can read more on this topic in Roy Gane's book *Altar Call.*

[5] Ellen G. White, *Testimonies for the Church,* vol. 5, p. 743.

[6] For a very down-home treatment of grace and justification by faith, see chapters 11-13 of my book *Journey of Joy* (Hagerstown, Md.: Review and Herald Pub. Assn., 1997).

[7] White, *Gospel Workers,* pp. 112, 113.

[8] White, *Christ's Object Lessons,* p. 149.

▲

CHAPTER 23

POLISHING THE RIGHT THINGS

OUR RIGHT TO LOVE HIS APPEARING

"There is laid up for me a crown of righteousness, which the Lord,
the righteous judge, shall give me at that day: and not to me only,
but unto all them also that love his appearing."
—Paul to Timothy (and us)[1]

"Heaven is a bargain, however great the cost."
—Unknown[2]

AS AN 8-YEAR OLD, ONE OF MY FAMILY CHORES was polishing the family's shoes for church each week. It was not my favorite job! On one particular day I carted them all out to the garage and set them on newspaper spread about the cement floor.

Next I climbed up the stepladder and pulled down from the shelf four bottles of shoe polish. Black for my Mary Janes, white for my mother's heels, brown for my little brother's tie-on shoes, and the final bottle, identified as "Cordovan," for my father's size 11 wing tips.

I unscrewed the cap of this last bottle and pulled out the woolen polishing puff ball—attached to the other end of the wire inside the lid. Suddenly I had an idea. Carefully I painted two fingernails cordovan brown and held out my hand.

H'mmmm, I thought, *cordovan has a lot of red in it—it kind of looks like fingernail polish. Pretty glamorous! I look like I have movie star hands,* I thought, eyeing the mop-up rag in case I heard Mother come out the back door of the house (she didn't approve of nail polish).

With the nails painted on one hand, I started on the other ones.

Suddenly, out of nowhere Mother magically appeared in the doorway of the garage. I had eight *fingernails* polished instead of eight shoes! At that moment my mother was the last person I wanted to see!

"Young lady, what do you think you're doing?"

It was too late to save myself.

The apostle Paul wrote to church leader Timothy saying, "There is laid up for me a crown of righteousness, which the Lord, the righteous judge, shall give me at that day: and not to me only, but unto all them also that *love his appearing*" (2 Tim. 4:8).

The reason I didn't "love" my mother's "appearing" that afternoon was that she had come upon me doing something other than the task she'd left for me to do.

Panther

The most accomplished balance beam "gymnast" that I personally know is Pansy Panther. After our yellow tabby disappeared into the nearby woods, Priscilla (our shorthaired gray cat) became very lonely. I decided to remedy the situation by going to a local pet center and purchasing a nonpurebred kitten.

Out of a litter of four only one was still available for purchase.

"He's a little boy kitten in perfect health," the clerk told me, holding up the yowling ball of long black fur. "And we will pay for a free vet check when you take him."

I brought the kitten home to join Priscilla as the other half of our family's outdoor mousing team. We named the kitten Panther (because my husband wants a real one up in heaven). Panther was so rambunctious, "he" all but destroyed the pansies in our back deck flower boxes within the first week of homecoming.

A week later a veterinarian kindly informed me that the "little boy kitten in perfect health" was indeed a little girl kitten—with a severe case of ringworm under her long black fur.

So Panther became Pansy Panther. And I became the chairperson of the local ringworm committee (responsible for daily kitty cream treatments and weekly antifungal baths).

Neither Pansy nor I relished those antiringworm bath-bonding times. Yet she came to know me and understand that I was the main being that fed her, played with her, and put fresh water in her little blue bowl.

Now she follows me like a puppy whenever I'm outside. If the shadow of an overhead hawk sweeps across the driveway, she runs to me for safety. Often when I'm inside, she hangs around the back door. When I don't come out after a "reasonable" length of time, she stands on her hind legs and looks through the windows.

When I do go outside, guess what! She absolutely *loves* my appearing! She purrs, meows, rubs against my ankles, and plays with my shoelaces.

Likewise, if we appreciate and love Christ *now,* we will *also* love His appearing at the Second Coming. We will love His appearing because we know we'll finally experience Him as a very real presence, instead of experiencing Him largely through faith as we do now.

We will love the fact that nothing can ever separate us again (John 14:3)!

Victorian Lampshades That Swim

The Republic of Palau has become the Pacific Ocean center for coral reef studies and reef conservation for the twenty-first century. Not too long ago that country opened a national aquarium on the 129-square-mile island of Babelthuap, with an accompanying museum complete with living exhibits of growing coral and other sea life.

As we were touring this center during a recent short-term mission trip, one of these exhibits elicited from me squeals of delight. "Look at those darling things!" I exclaimed to my husband.

In one of the smaller aquarium tanks were what appeared to be myriads of satin-covered, golden-white Victorian lampshades. In apparent slow motion, these exquisite creatures glided up and down past one another in the cobalt-blue water. Invisible currents rippled the "hems" of their graceful domes like lacy fringes in a breeze.

The nonscientific name for these creatures is "nonstinging jellyfish." A write-up near their aquarium stated that, outside of this museum, these unique sea creatures live in only one other location—a freshwater lake high atop one of the mountains in the Palauan archipelago.

The sun shines into this high mountain lake, enabling photosynthesis to take place. Photosynthesis ensures the growth of a lake algae. As the jellyfish feed on the algae, this water plant gently brushes a kiss of gold on their ivory exterior, giving them their unique color.

What I found so fascinating about these jellyfish is that they don't congregate where the algae grows. Instead, early each morning these exquisite creatures congregate on the eastern side of the lake, as soon as the sun begins to rise.

As the sun climbs up out of the sea and moves across the heavens, the jellyfish follow the source of the sunbeams, feeding on algae as they go, and playing in the sunlight.

If you were to hike up to this lake and arrive about noon at a certain cove, you could go out into the water and actually swim with the freshwater jellyfish. They are there at this time of day because the sun is directly overhead. Evening finds the jellyfish congregated near the western shore, where the sun has led them.

Here's something else I found fascinating about these jellyfish that follow the sun—they do no harm to other creatures. While visiting Australia a few weeks later, we couldn't even swim in the ocean because of the aggressive and poisonous jellyfish moving through that time of year. In fact, the hotel at which we stayed had mounted large containers of jellyfish-sting antidotes right next to the ocean-side gate of the fence for first aid should anyone be stung by these jellyfish. Victims who don't immediately apply the antidote risk a quick, painful death.

Yet the jellyfish that follow the sun are too busy staying in the direct rays to hurt anyone else. When darkness comes at night, these gentle jellyfish patiently wait out the night until the sun's next appearing draws them to the eastern shore.

When we learn to follow the rays of the Son of righteousness we too will do nothing that harms others. We too will awake each morning with a deep anticipation of and love for His soon appearing.

Do you remember that early morning by the Sea of Galilee soon after Christ's resurrection? Peter, the disciple who had asked Christ *not* to wash his feet in the upper room—the disciple who had denied Jesus three times—was fishing. He was also awaiting the next appearing of the Master whom he now loved—at last—more than himself.

A lone man standing on the shore caught Peter's attention. The man called out to Peter and his fellow fishermen. Suddenly Peter recognized the Man. Not able to contain himself, Peter plunged into the lake.

With swift strokes, he swam, as do those freshwater jellyfish, to the side of the lake where he could be warmed by the appearance of the risen Son (John 21:5-7).

Eclipses of the Son

I'm sure that being in the continual presence of the Son is our heart's desire, as it was Peter's. Yet, what about those times when a "dark surprise" obliterates the Son from our spiritual view?

What do we do when a sudden loss threatens to cast us from life's balance beam into the abyss of emotional and spiritual darkness? What do we do when the Son of righteousness "hides" behind the eclipse of life's tragedies?

Several years back my 85-year-old father said, "I want to go back to the Midwest one more time. In the fall of the year when I can see the changing leaves on the trees." At the time he said that my dad was recovering from open-heart surgery, which he'd had six months earlier.

My husband, being the way he is, immediately said, "Well, Dad, just get well. We'll take you back next year to see the fall colors."

Several months later I flew down to California, planning to spend time with my newly hospitalized father. Dad had been telling my brother and me to wait at least another week to come, until it was closer to my son's wedding. Yet both my brother and I decided to go a week earlier than scheduled in order to surprise Dad.

For the first time in a number of years I got my hair cut short into a style Dad would like. I made sure to pack a couple of pantsuits on which he always complimented me. I could almost anticipate his big hand in mine and I looked forward to sharing face to face.

Instead of surprising Dad, however, he surprised us. He died while we were en route. A family friend, blinking back tears, met us at the airport with the numbing news. I couldn't get my mind around what she was telling us. Dad was gone!

The following day terrorists, using airliner "bombs" with

human cargo, flew into the World Trade Center and the Pentagon. On Friday, three pain-filled days later, my father's memorial service just happened to coincide with our national day of mourning.

At my son's beautiful outdoor wedding barely a week later, I sat under the colorful autumn leaves that my father would have so dearly loved. My emotions felt as if they were in a blender. I didn't know if the tears trying to fall were those of intense happiness for my son and his beautiful new wife or of deep anguish over the loss of my father, who had hoped to be at their wedding.

One preacher, in a sermon following "Terrorist Tuesday," September 11, 2001, made this statement: "Life is not the way it's suppose to be; it's the way it is. How we *cope* with it is what makes the difference."

More and more, God is teaching me to cope with life's dark surprises in the light of His appearing. As He leads me to reflect on His appearing I am learning, more and more, to love the very thought of it.

For it is His appearing that will right all wrongs (Ps. 50:3, 4; Rom. 12:19).

His appearing will reunite us with loved ones (1 Thess. 4:13-18).

His appearing will change our mortality into immortality (1 Cor. 15:54).

His appearing will wipe away all tears (Rev. 21:4).

In Love With His Appearing

We will love His appearing because we have learned to go to sleep each night looking toward the place where we last saw the light.

We will truly love His appearing if, like those freshwater jellyfish, we have been greeting Him each morning on the eastern shore.

We will love His appearing if we have longed for it, prepared for it, and patiently waited for it (2 Thess. 3:5).

A love for His appearing reminds us to get back—spiritually speaking—to polishing the shoes instead of the fingernails. It excites us to work for the glory of the kingdom instead of our own.

At the most practical level, exercising our right to love His appearing steadies our feet on life's balance beam and is one of the most effective balancing techniques I know.

HOMEWORK FOR THE HEART

Nurturing a Love of His Appearing. If you aren't feeling real excited about Christ's second coming right now, you might want to take a closer look at your nails—er, rather your choices. (Remember that submission is an ongoing choice.)

Or perhaps, as I've noticed in my own experience, my intensity of anticipation for the Second Coming has a lot to do with my daily "swimming" patterns. Like the jellyfish, I would die spiritually without the Son to warm and guide me.

As the jellyfish feed on the sun-enhanced algae, I must also continually feed on the bread of life through promises such as 1 Corinthians 1:4-8, given specifically to those who joyfully wait for His appearing.

Note another Bible promise that deepens your love for His appearing: _____

_____ .

What, specifically, is it about this promise that makes you want to see Jesus come soon?

Reminder: The kind of relationship we have with the Son now will determine whether or not we will "love His appearing" when He returns.

---

[1] 2 Tim. 4:8.
[2] E. C. McKenzie. *14,000 Quips and Quotes*, p. 234.

CHAPTER 24

▲

WHEN LIFE LETS US DOWN

OUR RIGHT TO BE STILL

"Be still, and know that I am God."
—God, to King David[1]

IN PART 1 OF THIS BOOK we discussed ways to experience better balance in our lives by learning from the examples of balance in Christ's life. In Part 2 we have been discussing some of the rights God has given His "gymnasts" to exercise as they move across life's balance beam.

Most of us are goers and doers. As with me, perhaps you are genetically predisposed to activity. I want everything in my life to unfold in fast-forward. I'm not interested in red stoplights between home and the grocery store—or people standing in the checkout line ahead of me.

Sometimes, however, things happen. Horrible, cruel, unfair things happen on this sin-plagued, off-kilter planet that interrupt—even threaten to arrest—our progress toward the distant end of life's balance beam. These "things" can be anything from a debilitating automobile accident or the onset of a terminal disease to divorce or the death of a loved one.

When these tragic events blast away at the familiarity and comfort of our everyday world, does it mean that we are destined to be forever hurled from the balance beam? Are we never to experience equilibrium again?

Before we let the Bible answer these questions, let me set the stage with an account of a basketball game, and then introduce you to a dear friend of mine.

Pep Talk

At a school where I once taught, Ginnie,[2] the girls' physical education teacher, put together a faculty women's softball team for an after-school exposition game.

The student all-star team won the coin toss and chose to bat first. The first heavy hitter slammed the ball straight toward me. I was playing shortstop—but looking elsewhere. Yet somehow that big ball smacked right into my randomly open glove—and stayed there!

My teammates screamed in approval. Astounded students gasped in my direction with a new respect. For the rest of the game I miraculously did nothing to lose that respect.

A few days later the physical education teacher once again approached me. "Carolyn, I had no idea an English teacher could be such a great sportswoman. You're a pretty tough little cookie on the baseball diamond. How about playing center on the faculty women's team I'm putting together for alumni weekend?"

"Oh, I don't *do* basketball," I truthfully responded. But somehow she cajoled me into saying yes to her request.

At our two pregame practices, Ginnie became increasingly sober as I missed basket after basket. She realized my response to her invitation had *not* been based on false modesty; I just couldn't sink basketballs into the hoop. Furthermore, I was no better anywhere else on the court.

"Carolyn, stay on top of your opponent!" she kept yelling. My powerless throws to teammates missed their marks. I lost count of the times I fumbled.

"Ginnie," I said at the end of practice one day, "may I please speak to you privately?" When the others were out of earshot, I said, "Look, this team would be stronger without me. Why don't you just quietly drop me?"

She looked hard at me through her perspiration-splattered glasses. "Let me put it to you this way. I'm shorthanded. So, believe it or not, I actually *need* you."

"Whoa," I sighed, disappointed she wasn't going to let me off the hook. "I can't imagine how I could possibly help."

"I can't either," she said with the hint of a twinkle in her eye. "But I do have an idea. In the game next weekend, don't think of yourself as a center anymore."

"OK," I said. "How should I think of myself?"

Ginnie took a deep breath before answering. "I'm going to put this to you as kindly as I can. Try to think of yourself as a warm body—even a big blob—that sort of stands around on the court and gets in the way of all the opponents."

"OK," I said, trying to hide my sense of humiliation.

"Oh," she said as an afterthought, "if one of our teammates accidentally throws you the ball—but I'll warn them not to—get rid of it immediately! Let your teammates win the game. You hold back and be still, except for the warm body big-blob part."

Being Still

Wow, what a pep talk! Now I dreaded the upcoming game more than ever.

Before the game (probably to intimidate our strong, youthful opponents) Ginnie grouped our team in a circle for a little pregame chant. Though my heart wasn't in it, I contributed the "Go team!" thing at the end with my teammates.

Then my teammates moved into position. Someone suddenly vise-gripped my arm. Ginnie stage-whispered into my ear, "Remember . . . *warm body* on the court. *Big blob* that's always in the way. But let the *others* handle the ball!"

The next hour was a blur of on- and off-court frenzy while students screamed and Ginnie shouted instructions. My teammates kept sinking balls into the hoop. I remember that I did a lot of random floating on the court while a lot of people bumped into me.

In fact, I felt a little roughed up by the time the ref blew the final whistle. Yet at the end of the game the student team conceded loss and we graciously shook their hands. The euphoric Ginnie patted us each on the back with individual commendations.

"Brenda, ball of fire, you go, girl!"

"Great shots, Norma!"

"Karen, fabulous defense!"

Then she moved in close to my face, beaming. "Carolyn," she said in a low voice, "you stood *still* at all the right times—and *let* us win! You were *awesome!*"

Letting God Carry the Ball

Perhaps when the cruel blows of life weaken us and threaten to knock us off the balance beam, God might sometimes just want us to stand still so that He can "carry the ball" for a while. When we prayerfully follow His coaching—even when it hurts our pride—He is often able to accomplish what we'd never be capable of doing for ourselves.

In fact, many others have learned this lesson before me.

A prophet of God once told Judah's King Jehoshaphat about an upcoming battle, "Stand ye still," he said, "and see the salvation of the Lord with you" (2 Chron. 20:17). On another occasion God said to Isaiah about the Egyptians, "Their strength is to sit still" (Isa. 30:7)!

Perhaps the apostle Paul was feeling at a disadvantage the day he wrote, "Most gladly I will rather boast in my infirmities, that the power of Christ may rest upon me" (2 Cor. 12:9, NKJV). After all, God Himself had told Paul, "My grace is sufficient for you, for my power is made perfect in weakness" (verse 9, NIV).

Lucy

And then there's Lucy—she's one of the most perfectly balanced people I know. She is *so* going forward on the balance beam—all the time. On some days, even her uplifting, energetic e-mails just keep *me* going!

For whatever reason, God has been allowing Lucy, my friend and former classmate, to experience overwhelming tragedy in her life. Since her early 20s Lucy has suffered terribly from crippling arthritis. For years she has had to support her bent frame with crutches as she walks on crippled legs. Lucy refers to her physical appearance as "deformed."

In addition, Lucy is blind in one eye. Throughout her life she has also suffered emotionally at the hands of others who really didn't care. For years, until the pain and disabilities forced Lucy to take an early retirement, she still made her life count for others—through teaching and social work.

Not long ago, however, Lucy admitted herself into an emergency room with severe nausea and stomach pain. In her own words she describes, "I was in the hospital for that particular week under observation for the 'flu' and then sent home with antibiotics."

After vomiting for a week, Lucy—her weight by then down to 61 pounds—was seen at the hospital by a specialist. After doing a CAT scan, he rushed her into surgery for an appendectomy. Lucy would have been dead days before if scar tissue from a previous surgery hadn't encapsulated her ruptured appendix.

To make a long story short, the previous week of constant vomiting permanently eroded Lucy's esophagus. She could no longer take in food through her mouth. She was in so much physical pain that she pleaded with doctors and friends just to pull the GI tube and allow her to die.

Lucy shared, "I was in a combination of three hospitals and one nursing home during the six-week-long ordeal." Doctors finally removed the GI tube but replaced it with a permanent feeding tube into Lucy's stomach. Then they released her to a nursing home.

She has recovered enough to live in her own apartment but must have a caregiver come in twice daily to do for her what she cannot do for herself. Lucy's movements are limited to the length of the cord on her feeder machine. She says it takes forever to get from one location to another, since she has to both push her feeder pole and still walk with crutches.

One caregiver became so impatient with Lucy's disabilities that she physically charged at Lucy, sending her back to the hospital because her fragile nervous system couldn't handle this stress.

Experiencing shock, anguish, and then despondency, Lucy—like Job's wife—was tempted many times to question God's love for her. Surely she had fallen, permanently, from life's balance beam, with no hope of ever getting back up on it again.

Yet, back in her apartment again, Lucy decided to do whatever it took to become vertical on the balance beam, her hand firmly in God's.

She sent me an e-mail about what subsequently took place and has given me permission to share it with you.

"A week ago Sabbath I decided to spend it in total silence—no music, no Christian radio, no Christian TV—and just listen for what God might want to tell me.

"The first insight that came was that I was grumbling about my feeding tube just like the children of Israel grumbled in the wilderness. I decided to accept my feeding tube as God's manna from heaven for this wilderness time of mine.

"The second revelation was that I really resent having to have caregivers. I am so fiercely independent. I really have a hard time when they 'mess up,' don't show, etc. I decided that I need to change my attitude toward them and see them as my 'angels unawares' sent by God to care for me. . . .

"I realized that even though the route to healing was forgiveness, I hadn't forgiven the doctors yet. I had to ask God for the ability to forgive them. . . .

"Yesterday was the icing on the cake of revelations. It took a long time before I could accept myself or feel acceptable to God because of my deformities. The subtle message given to me by the 'church' [when I was] growing up was that if you lived right you wouldn't get a disease like this. I figured I had somehow done something to deserve such punishment. Then I came across Psalm 147:10, 11. It reads, 'His pleasure is not in the strength of the horse, nor his delight in the legs of a man; the Lord delights in those who fear him, who put their hope in his unfailing love' [NIV]. I decided that if my weakness and deformities didn't offend God, then I wouldn't be offended by them either. It was still a struggle to think that God would choose to live in this damaged temple, but I finally accepted that He would and invited Him to take up residence.

"I feel so full of joy for the first time since before my illness.

"Love, Lucy."

Your Unique Walk

Lucy's experience only reminds us of the conclusion to which we keep returning in our discussion on balance. True balance is really about your and my one-on-one relationship with God—no matter what!

God has a special walk for each of us on our own unique balance beam. Some of us may advance gracefully from start to finish. The majority of us, however, spend a lot of time falling off and getting back on.

Some advance quickly; others tentatively.

Some of us are strong and healthy; others are weak or sick.

For all of us, however, come those times in our lives when our walk on the balance beam comes to a temporary halt. In those seasons of perplexity, grief, anxiety, loss, anger, or fear, our best choice may be to simply stand still and cling to the strong hand of the one who loves us best.

At those times, in particular, God calls us to rest, to lean on Him. "In returning and rest shall ye be saved; in quietness and in confidence shall be your strength" (Isa. 30:15).

No matter what or who in life has let us down—we can know that "the Lord thy God in the midst of thee is mighty; he will save" (Zeph. 3:17).

HOMEWORK FOR THE HEART

Being Still. As I briefly mentioned earlier, I've been recently diagnosed with breast cancer. Medical appointments and treatments have turned my lifestyle upside down—not to mention that of my husband's, as well.

In addition to fervent prayer and leaning on God's promises for guidance and strength, we are also learning to "be still" in other ways. For example, we are taking advantage of various other resources, which I believe are secondary gifts from God: a professional support group, helpful friends, the wisdom to cut back, temporarily we hope, on our heavy family and church commitments.

Might something in your life seem overwhelming right now?

What promises might you claim for this situation? What support options outside yourself could you tap into that would allow you to "be still" long enough to regroup?

Reminder: In times when normal "balance" seems out of the question and beyond our control, we can be still (in various ways) and trust the mighty hand of God to steady us.

---

[1] Ps. 46:10.

[2] Not her real name.

CHAPTER 25

PEACE ON THE BALANCE BEAM

OUR RIGHT TO CLAIM HIGHER GROUND

*"I press toward the mark for the prize
of the high calling of God in Christ Jesus."*
—Paul to the Philippians[1]

A MAGAZINE ADVERTISEMENT I RECENTLY READ indicates how out of balance we can become in an off-kilter world.

"Don't let unwanted calls interrupt your favorite shows or movies!" the advertisement implored readers. The ad then described how a new product enables a television viewer to store—in a caller log displayed right across the television screen—up to 14 phone calls without interrupting the viewing of his favorite sitcom or sports event.[2]

How rude! we might think. *Who'd be so selfish as to block out attempts by family or friends to get in touch and, even possibly, for reasons of emergency?*

Yet, how often have we been so wrapped up in trying to do our own thing—whether it's pleasure or rush mode business as usual—that we've forced God to leave His messages in our "caller log"?

What an opposite response Christ has when we call upon Him! Not only is He waiting to hear from us, He also continues to search us out, as He sought out each disciple in the upper room that evening so long ago.

Feeling His Pull

My rubber flip-flops slapped poufs of dust behind me as I trudged along the unpaved African road. The ruffle at the bottom of my long skirt swished back and forth, flashing rhythmic glimpses of dirty feet. Squawking chickens ran out of my path as I made my way up the winding hill toward the home of my student. Her family had invited me to spend the night.

The first three hours of this trip found me riding in the back of a bouncing pickup truck under the equatorial sun. Now, with eyes full of dusty grit, I finished the last half hour of the trip on foot.

By the time I arrived at their mud-brick house overlooking the sun-dried city below, the strap of my woven plastic bag was cutting into my shoulder. My parched throat felt like sandpaper. Even blinking was miserable.

Family members greeted me with the traditional hug and led me to a rough-hewn backless bench in a cool, dark room with one small window. A younger sister of my student slipped into the room carrying a bottle of orange soda. Shyly she placed it on the table before me and opened it with a little bottle opener.

The wooden door creaked again as, this time, my student pushed it open. Stooping, she placed two objects before me on the earthen floor: a pitcher of water and a basin. A towel lay across one shoulder, and she held a bar of soap in her hand.

Just for a moment—halfway around the world—the scenario transported me in my mind's eye to the upper room of 2,000 years ago.

At that moment—as the cool, cleansing water splashed across my feet—I had a deeper sense of what it means to be an unworthy disciple whom God chooses to love anyway.

As I left for home the next day, I knew God had refreshed me for a steadier walk in service for Him.

Many years have passed since that real-life foot washing. Many people, places, and even purposes in my life have changed—at times plunging me into a state of panic. Yet, with each trauma, loss, or uncertainty, God has always called me back to the upper room.

In the upper room . . . I again encounter Christ on His knees before me, ministering to my needs and showing me (no matter what's going on in my life) that I can always move forward on the balance beam as long as I keep Him close.

In the upper room . . . I always struggle—as did the distraught

Peter—between God's will and mine. In those times that I turn my will over to Him and He replaces the panic with peace, I always wonder what took me so long.

The Servant of servants and Lord of lords has always pulled me to my spiritual feet and into a vertical position again. Even when hot tears—induced by divorce, death of a loved one, or a cancer diagnosis—were blinding me.

Then He has faithfully and tenderly lifted me back up on the balance beam. There, with His hand firmly holding mine, He has continued to lead me—journeying somewhere between heaven and earth—toward the place He is preparing for my eternal rest (Ex. 23:20; John 14:2, 3).

No, the balance beam under our feet will not always *feel* solid. More often than not, it will *feel* shaky. That's because God asks us to walk by faith, not by our emotions or by what is going on around us (Ps. 23:4-6; 46:1-3, 7).

Yes, at times we may be in great physical or emotional pain while teetering above the garbage of this dying planet. Yet with each step He leads us to take, He enables our feeble declaration, enunciated by the apostle Paul so many years ago, "None of these things move me" (Acts 20:24).

I don't know about you, but I'm with the writer of this old hymn:
> "I want to live above the world,
> Though Satan's darts at me are hurled;
> For faith has caught the joyful sound,
> The song of saints on higher ground.
> Lord, lift me up, and I shall stand
> By *faith,* on heaven's tableland;
> A higher plain than I have found;
> Lord, plant my feet on higher ground."[3]

The believer has the right to ask God to plant her feet on higher ground. "The steps of a good man," wrote King David, "are ordered by the Lord. . . . Though he fall, he shall not be utterly cast down: for the Lord upholdeth him with his hand. . . . None of his steps shall slide" (Ps. 37:23-31).

When God has us by the hand and is walking beside us on His

balance beam toward the kingdom, you and I have the inalienable right to . . .

- *resist* the enemy.
- *breathe* in the Father's forgiveness.
- *persist* in His will.
- *discern, love,* and *apply* His truth.
- *be* as *holy* in our domain as He is in His.
- *love His appearing.*
- *be still* when we're too weak to do anything else.
- *claim higher ground.*

You and I have *God's authority* to exercise these rights! Why? Because His plan of salvation, culminating with the cross on Mount Calvary, has already entitled us to another foundational right: that of being in an all-consuming love relationship with the Lamb of God.

Taking Advantage

What eternal fools we would be not to take advantage of our second chances to walk by faith on our balance beams! What fools *not* to press on the upward way—despite the disequilibrium in this off-kilter world!

I suspect that the closer I get to heaven, the more I'll be able to feel—by faith—the Savior's steadying hand around mine.

The closer I get, the better I'll see His other hand grasping *yours* as we each emerge on our converging balance beams—far above worldly imbalance—into heaven's diaphanous mists.

With the Savior walking between us, holding our hands, we'll look up from our weary feet to the destination just a short space ahead.

There, in the diffused glory shining from the throne, stands the Ancient of Days, arms outstretched and shedding tears (like the father of the prodigal) of joy, anticipation, and excitement.

Glancing down at our feet one final time, we'll be amazed to discover that these balance beams, which had their shaky beginnings mired in a dark world, have become thick, sturdy beams of golden light shining from the throne!

O, precious friend, go forward on God's balance beam! Go! The Father is waiting to empower your walk of faith toward better balance in Him. Claim peace now and then higher ground in just a little while.

I know that neither of us wants to miss out on that last step. With our hands still in the Savior's, we'll leap from our respective beams of light into the eternal comfort of the Father's arms.

Enfolded in glory, we hear, close to our ears, His words: "This is why I created you in the first place" (see Rev. 4:11). As He sings over us, the anthem reverberates throughout the universe. With tenderness and a love that wants to gaze into our eyes throughout eternity, He at last sets our eternally youthful feet onto solid celestial ground.

Did you know that all of heaven longs for this day?

Do you?

Do I?

Then, equipped with promises of hope, let's press forward on the balance beam. Fortified by faith, let's confidently, purposefully place one foot in front of the other, knowing that nothing occurring in our lives or in the world will be able to misdirect our steps or cast us to the ground.

As fellow gymnasts on the Lord's team, let's cheer one another on: "Fear thou not . . ., Let not thine hands be slack. The Lord thy God in the midst of thee is mighty; he will save, he will rejoice over thee with joy; he will rest in his love, he will joy over thee with singing" (Zeph. 3:16, 17).

Until the day we take that final step into eternity, let us stay vertical. Let us live above the world.

Let us claim—and press upward toward—higher ground.

Even in an off-kilter world, we can advance, ever forward on the balance beam!

Reminder: No matter what is going on in our lives now, God gives us the authority to claim higher ground for both His glory as well as for our eternal good.

---

[1] Phil. 3:14.

[2] *Sky Mall* ad (SourceCode: 1DQX244, Alaska Airlines *Sky Mall* catalog).

[3] Charles H. Gabriel, "Higher Ground," *The Seventh-day Adventist Hymnal* (Hagerstown, Md.: Review and Herald Pub. Assn., 1985), No. 625. (Italics supplied.)